WRITE TO THE TOP!

WRITE TO THE TOP!
HOW TO BECOME A PROLIFIC ACADEMIC

W. Brad Johnson

=

Carol A. Mullen

WRITE TO THE TOP!
© W. Brad Johnson and Carol A. Mullen, 2007.

First published in 2007 by
PALGRAVE MACMILLAN™
175 Fifth Avenue, New York, N.Y. 10010 and
Houndmills, Basingstoke, Hampshire, England RG21 6XS
Companies and representatives throughout the world.

PALGRAVE MACMILLAN is the global academic imprint of the Palgrave Macmillan division of St. Martin's Press, LLC and of Palgrave Macmillan Ltd. Macmillan® is a registered trademark in the United States, United Kingdom and other countries. Palgrave is a registered trademark in the European Union and other countries.

ISBN-13: 978–1–4039–7742–7 hardcover
ISBN-10: 1–4039–7742–9   hardcover
ISBN-13: 978–1–4039–7743–4 paperback
ISBN-10: 1–4039–7743–7   paperback

Library of Congress Cataloging-in-Publication Data

Johnson, Brad W.
   Write to the top! : how to become a prolific academic / W. Brad Johnson and Carol A. Mullen.
      p. cm.
   Includes bibliographical references and index.
   ISBN 1–4039–7742–9 hardcover (alk. Paper)—ISBN 1–4039–7743–7 paperback (alk. Paper)
      1. Academic writing. 2. English language—Rhetoric I. Mullen, Carol A. II. Title.

P301.5.A27J64 2007
808'.042—dc22   2006051550

A catalogue record for this book is available from the British Library.

Design by Newgen Imaging Systems (P) Ltd., Chennai, India.

First edition: June 2007

10 9 8 7 6 5 4 3 2 1

Printed in the United States of America.

Transferred to Digital Printing 2008

This book is dedicated to all who strive to become prolific writers in the academy

Contents

Acknowledgments

We offer a heartfelt thanks to Amanda Johnson, acquisitions editor at Palgrave Macmillan. Amanda showed immediate interest in our idea for this book and urged us on, carrying it through both the internal and external review phases. Her steadfast support along with that of her team has made this project that much more pleasurable.

We are also indebted to several good friends and writing colleagues. Over the years, their loyal and energetic partnerships have helped to make us both productive academics. Without their inspirational ideas, hard work, and personal support, our writing lives would be lonely indeed. Brad Johnson thanks Clark Campbell, Mark Eastburg, Albert Ellis, Greg Harper, Jennifer Huwe, William Johnson, Rocky Lall, Kelly Murray, Steve Nielsen, and Charles Ridley. Carol Mullen is grateful to, among others, Jean Clandinin, Theodore Creighton, Patrick Diamond, Fenwick English, Sandra Harris, Patrick Jenlink, William Kealy, Joe Kincheloe, Frances Kochan, Chris Myers, Thomas Nelson, Ulrich Reitzug, and Shirley Steinberg. And because both of us are fast approaching the full professor milestone, we want to acknowledge the faculty-minded spirit of our superb and supportive academic deans—William Miller of the United States Naval Academy and Colleen Kennedy of the University of South Florida.

Finally, we thank our families and students for their persistent patience, understanding, and cheerleading. Your steadfast support as we labor at our keyboards makes the academic life more palatable, often even a joy.

PREFACE

This brief guide to writing is designed to help any academic become not only productive, but truly prolific. By prolific we mean writing and publishing a great deal and generally beyond even the most rigorous university norms for productive scholarship. It is a pithy, no-nonsense, no-excuses guide to maximizing both the quality and quantity of your scholarly products. *Write to the Top!* offers a concise overview of the art and science of writing efficiently and effectively; it is your one-stop source for the nuts and bolts of success in getting things written and into print, and for navigating the cultural-and-editorial mountain along the way. This is the first book that explicitly summarizes the key elements to prolific productivity in academic settings. It is also the first text that translates the hidden curriculum of the academy's cultural mores into transparent lessons. Each chapter is constructed around several secrets to writing productivity and success, and each integrates the personal and professional dimensions of writing.

Each year, thousands of newly minted doctorates enter the halls of academe—newcomers eager but naïve regarding the overwhelming demands to teach, serve the institution, and patiently mentor students. And there is more: Foreboding rumors about the demand for publications and ominous whispers about predecessors who, failing to publish adequately, were ignobly shown to the exit by unimpressed tenure committees and university administrators. Like the proverbial deer in the headlights, these early career professors risk becoming frozen in place as the tenure-and-promotion milestones bear down with terrifying rapidity. Until now, there has been no single source of advice about how to get immediately started on the writing—we estimate this to be 90 percent of the battle for many new academics—and how to craft an approach to scholarship that heightens the probability of sustained success as an author. In this guide, we hope to help new professors in higher education, regardless of their discipline, college, and institution, plot a course of productive writing and stick with it.

We also have another group of colleagues in mind as our audience for this guide. *Write to the Top!* should be a source of comfort, encouragement, and pragmatic advice to more advanced academics who, for any number of reasons, have failed to consistently produce and now search for straightforward solutions. Whether the factors contributing to low productivity are structural, institutional, cultural, behavioral, interpersonal, personal, or emotional in nature, this guide takes systematic aim at each. Still another peer group for whom this guide will prove useful includes those seasoned professors who are tenured and successful, but genuinely interested in learning some new strategies for streamlining their writing habits and increasing both output and enjoyment of the scholarly enterprise. These writing veterans who might also be entering a generative stage of their careers may find themselves in need of a tool for "restarting their engines."

Yet another group of colleagues for whom this book was designed are seasoned faculty who either formally or informally mentor junior colleagues and graduate students in their research and writing. Having a guide on hand that one can easily consult in the effort to support one's younger counterparts and protégés can prove reassuring, especially where advice, strategies, and tips for effective partnership and productive writing are all primed for just such uses.

A final group of primary consumers for this work are department heads, academic deans, formal mentors, diversity directors, and other faculty developers who want to give new faculty members an edge when it comes to successfully meeting institutional and disciplinary demands for scholarly productivity. If it is the job of these institutional leaders to guide and support new scholars as they learn the secrets to successful productivity, this book should make their work considerably easier.

Our interest in prolific writing as a subject of discourse stems from several sources. First, both of us are very busy, productive writers. We have each been immersed in the writing life for many years and together have authored more than 200 peer-reviewed scholarly works and 17 books. We both love the act of writing, experiencing it as simultaneously mind-expanding, challenging, and intrinsically rewarding; we still find that successfully getting our work in print is deeply satisfying. This is probably the result of a higher-than-average need for achievement, a predilection toward creativity, and more than our share of obsessive-compulsiveness. Familiar with one another's work on the topic of mentoring, and always impressed that the other could produce so much excellent scholarship each year, we began an informal dialogue about the "secrets" to success as writers. We wondered why so many of our colleagues struggled with this salient aspect of professorial life, and what it was that made prolific scholars shine. Over the years, colleagues and even academics unknown to us have approached us about how it is that we produce so much, asking, "What's your secret?" This question served as yet another catalyst prompting our formulation of the idea for this book.

Based on our interchanges with each other and other prolific academics, the need for a pithy and clear guide to the secrets of being prolific in the professorate came into view. As seasoned authors and experienced editors, we had some good ideas about the key elements of writing success but we also began to review published literature, talk informally with other authors, and even conduct empirical research on the qualities and behaviors of outrageously productive scholars. We also drew from our experiences as advisors and mentors to a generation of graduate students in clinical psychology (Johnson) and educational leadership (Mullen). Perhaps nothing helps to more clearly define the elements of successful and unsuccessful writing than reading early drafts of beginning writers' efforts. We worked equally hard at the book and envisioned ourselves as equal to the task from the outset. Borrowing from an alternative form of partnership developed and published by Carol Mullen and colleague Frances Kochan, we placed an equal sign (=) between our names as authors of this book to signal the status of our partnership. This book is the net outcome of a sustained personal and professional journey to reveal the keys to successful academic productivity, written by faculty for faculty and advanced students.

This is a short guide. Modeled on the efficient beauty of Strunk and White's (2000) timeless classic, *The Elements of Style, Write to the Top!* avoids lengthy narrative and gets right to the heart of each secret to writing success. We have distilled voluminous experience, advice, and empirical evidence down to 65 secrets to prolific writing. These secrets are clustered within the following eleven chapters—each with a core theme:

1. Establish a well-honed writing habit
2. Become dogmatically disciplined and set firm boundaries
3. Cater to your writing rhythms
4. Develop the attitudes and perspectives of a prolific scholar
5. Know when to collaborate and when to cut losses
6. Practice systematic writing from start to finish
7. Revise, edit, and revise some more
8. Seek mentors, mentoring networks, and writing coaches
9. Tackle thoughts and emotions that block productivity
10. Master the mechanics of publication
11. Drink deeply from the cup of life

Becoming a prolific writer is no easy task. It demands long hours, unflinching commitment, and the capacity to delay gratification while keeping eyes locked on the goal. Prolific professors tend to get started early in their careers and they make writing a central component of their scholarly identities. Becoming a successful academic author can be lonely and agonizing; it can also be engaging, fraught with meaning, and occasionally, even thrilling. Whether you are a graduate student preparing for an academic career, a new professor, or a seasoned writer in search of a tool for encouraging junior colleagues, we hope that *Write to the Top!* serves as a crucial guide on the road to outrageous productivity.

W. Brad Johnson   =   Carol A. Mullen
Annapolis, Maryland   Tampa, Florida

1

FIRST, ESTABLISH A WELL-HONED WRITING HABIT

Here is where it all begins: Deciding to write. With this hurdle in the rearview mirror, the rest of the journey to prolific writing is just about the details. In this chapter, we highlight the crucial foundation to a productive professorial life. After making a decision to become prolific in your chosen field, you will need to weave the act of writing into the fabric of your scholarly identity and find an interesting academic niche that so intrigues and satisfies that you have a reasonably good chance of remaining intrigued and satisfied through the early phase of your career. At the outset, new academics must seize control of their schedules, block chunks of time for writing, and commit to a daily writing regimen. But more, they must also be prepared to maximize unanticipated down time each day—understanding that an hour waiting for a child's athletic practice to end could be an hour well spent proofreading a draft, outlining an article, or just jotting down thoughts or a scholarly "to-do" list. Finally, making writing a well-honed habit requires a commitment to both secure and then maximize longer writing retreats. Prolific academics quickly discover the beauty of sequestered writing days and they guard them jealously without becoming delinquent under the pressure of other responsibilities.

1   WRITE OR DON'T WRITE BUT MAKE A DECISION

You can decide to undertake the prolific writer's life, or to have a career other than college professor. Whatever your choice, make it authentic and true to who you are and want to become.

There it is. If academic writing or scholarship production in your discipline is excruciating, unrewarding, or inherently disinteresting, then we solemnly absolve you of the burden of a career in academe. You may be someone who could never commit to academic productivity simply because the scholarly life is not your calling. Although you find yourself in academe, you sense that the act of creating scholarly contributions is likely to be a joyless, if not unrewarding endeavor. If this description rings true for you, we encourage you to put this book aside and go in another direction. Find another mountain to climb.

Higher education faculty must contribute to their disciplines through the production of original scholarship. In a word, they must write. Although specific definitions of productivity range widely across institutions, the assumption that professors shall produce before being tenured or promoted is as ironclad in academe as the notion that professors should teach. This is why it is essential that we are honest about our fit with academe. In an effort to be honest with oneself about this fit, one needs to understand one's personal motives for academic writing. In addition to "sheer egotism, aesthetic enthusiasm, historical impulse, and political purpose"—all of which can be considered pluses—one can also identify "professional advancement, the requirements of guild membership, [and] the psychic battle with one's teachers [or former mentors]" (Germano, 2006, p. B5). The latter reasons are the ones that haunt many of us late at night and they are probably futile and empty unless undergirded with some pluses. Rather than languish in a job that emphasizes an activity you can barely tolerate, let alone love, why not seek work in an institution that prizes teaching above all else or find a different way altogether to deploy your graduate degree?

As a reader of this guide, we assume that you are prepared to embark on a journey toward steadfast productivity as a scholarly writer. We applaud you. But as the title of this section suggests, you must first commit to doing the writing. Although many of the insider tips and secrets conveyed later will help to sharpen the quality and quantity of the writing, it will all be for naught if you don't decide here and now to make writing a habit.

As a famous purveyor of athletic footwear is fond of saying, "Just Do It."

Perhaps nothing sabotages new faculty more thoroughly than inaction with regard to writing. Overwhelmed with myriad responsibilities, the new faculty member can become frozen and unable to act while the competing demands of teaching, scholarship, service, and student advising bear down like a freight train. A paradox: Although it appears wise to defer scholarly pursuits until one has achieved some mastery of teaching, student relationships, and committee work, this is no wiser a move than waiting until midlife to begin saving for retirement. In fact, one could find creative ways to compensate in the latter scenario but not in the first—academic writing cannot be delayed without serious penalty. If your scholarly life is limping along or hanging in limbo, crucial evaluations of your performance show no mercy, and these will come at you full tilt. In most instances, you will have some kind of formal contract renewal evaluation known as mid-tenure review (or something similar) by the third year.

In light of the notorious lag times characteristic of peer-reviewed journals and book publishers, scholarly work submitted for publication in your second year is not likely to be published before your first review. Here is the translation: Unless you start writing immediately upon commencing an academic career, your third-year review may have the feel of one of those bad dreams in which you have gone to school naked, or failed to take a crucial exam. Because the demands for research productivity have escalated since the 1990s, even doctoral program graduates headed for tenure-track positions will do well to have some publications under their belt. There is much to learn and no time to spare when it comes to scholarly writing.

Of course, the same holds true for the traditional tenure-and- evaluation juncture—typically at the five or six-year mark. Unless you have made an earnest and binding commitment to write consistently—even in the earliest days of your career—you will have a difficult time demonstrating a steady flow of scholarly products (e.g., articles, books, book chapters).

There is one more reason to make writing a well-honed habit from day one, or at least from the moment you decide to read this guide: Producing scholarship inherently defines you as a scholar, just as enabling student learning defines you as a teacher. It is often difficult to effectively mentor students if you are unable to model current scholarly work or include novice researchers in the various phases of producing a paper or article. The most effective teachers and mentors are consummate scholars.

Start writing today. In fact, the act of deciding to write—forging a commitment to become prolific—is so fundamentally crucial to your ultimate success that we ask you to stop reading this guide for today. Put it aside for now and instead go do at least an hour of writing on a project that needs your attention. Pick the guide up again tomorrow; the remaining pages will be easier to read and will hold greater meaning if you come to them refreshed, as someone committing to writing.

2   WRITE AS A WAY OF LIFE

Now that you have decided to write, it is time to make academic writing a core element of your scholarly identity.

Too often, academics view scholarship as a necessary evil, an adjunctive activity to be tolerated and weathered out of sheer determination to get tenured or promoted. Seen through this lens, writing is a job, a demand, even a trial to be endured; like doing your taxes, cleaning the basement, or swallowing cough syrup, we force ourselves to do it in hopes of putting the nasty business behind us. From this angle, scholarship becomes drudgery, writing becomes labor, and any joy that might have once accompanied the process of creating academically is squashed. It is no surprise that one well-established research finding from the psychology of learning goes something like this: When external rewards (e.g., cash) are applied to an activity that a person does for pleasure (e.g., writing), that activity often decreases in frequency—its positive valence declines. What was once done for the love of the activity becomes tied to one's livelihood and thus associated with an onerous demand. Imagine your dean standing outside the door each day when you walked into teach, handing you a few twenties to compensate you for that day's work. Although the thought of this individual giving you money might be appealing on some level, you get the point; soon, teaching would begin to feel less like a vocation and more like a job. Slowly, extrinsic incentives would upstage intrinsic rewards.

Rather than conceive of writing merely as something you do—perhaps because academic leaders like your dean say you have to—we challenge you to integrate writing into the very center of who you are. If you want to become a prolific academic, then weave the act of writing into the fabric of your identity and the mosaic of your daily life. Writing must be something you do because it is core to who you are. As Germano (2006) says, "Nothing really explains why we write, but it's a sure thing that we try to put words together because of who each of us is" (B5). Even though sitting at the keyboard day after day is an act of doing, it is also a way of being and of continuing to be, and even of living our lives fully and to the end.

Remember, this is a guide to becoming a prolific academic. We are not envisioning you becoming the kind of professor who can produce a bit of scholarship merely to pass muster at promotion junctures. If you begin to love the act of writing, we predict that you will write a lot and write better and better. But for writing to really take hold in the far reaches of your sense of self, you must engage it as fully as you do other activities that are central to your being.

To accomplish this full integration of writing and being, you may need to undergo a major cognitive and emotional shift in the way you define yourself. It is time to start experiencing the act of writing as a soulful and meaning-generating activity. Like eating, sleeping, preparing for class, or taking care of your children, scholarship is something you need to do daily—eventually, without much premeditation or planning. When writing every day is simply assumed, when it has taken up residence in your unconscious daily scheduling, you will know that this transformative shift in perspective has occurred.

Prolific academics accept the fact that writing is not always sheer delight. For, it is simultaneously challenging, invigorating, frustrating, exhausting, and rewarding—much like teaching, marriage, or a host of other activities and commitments you treasure but that episodically stir discontent or even agony. When writing moves center stage, it will be hard to imagine your life and self without it. When it becomes part of your identity, when you truly experience some delight in the process of routinely turning thoughts and ideas into words and sentences, and when writing is an assumed activity upon waking in the morning, then the line between work and play starts dissolving. This is our wish for you: May writing become a way of life, and may scholarship become more joy than burden.

3   WRITE ABOUT WHAT COMPELS YOU

Writing can be exceptionally hard work. There will be days, nights, and weekends when you wonder what you've gotten yourself into. Deadlines loom, certain writing tasks become repetitive, and, without warning, the writing muse deserts you. This is why we implore you to find a scholarly niche compelling enough to sustain you through the tough spots; you need a topic that holds the promise of keeping you engaged—perhaps throughout the life of your academic writing career.

Those of us who mentor graduate students, and have the privilege of serving as thesis advisors and dissertation chairs, can be heard saying something like, "pick a topic you love—the work will be challenging enough without selecting an area that bores you." This is sage advice. It is even more apropos for the junior professor. Quite often, the most prolific academics are those who find an intriguing scholarly focus early in their careers and then stick with it for the long haul. When an academic becomes utterly immersed in an area of personal fascination, several important things happen: (a) work becomes play and writing is transformed into a natural expression of intellectual excitement; (b) with rather surprising rapidity, experience and cumulative contributions to the niche elevate the scholar to the status of expert; and (c) one's publication record bears the trademarks of a genuine scholar capable of sustaining an enduring line of programmatic research.

Because it is important to write about what compels you and to commit to this topic for the long term, marriage—or any monogamous partnership—offers an apt metaphor for this process. During the courtship phase, often during graduate school or very early in your career, consider those questions and topics that hold the power to stir, excite, delight, and intrigue, you—ward against mere infatuations. Remember, you are looking for the real thing, love. Substitutes are mere fancies and fads. When novelty and energy decline, will the topic you have carefully chosen be enough to sustain you? Have you found an intellectual quest you just might be happy enough to "grow old" with?

In fact, Robert Sternberg's (1986) *Triangular Theory of Love* offers an interesting extension of the marriage metaphor. He hypothesized three critical vectors in any love relationship: (a) *intimacy*—do you feel connected and bonded to the person (or in our case, the topic) and is there a genuine desire to pursue it at all costs? (b) *passion*—does the topic generate sincere attraction and drive, continuing to foment excitement even after the honeymoon phase? (c) *decision/ commitment*—can you make a short-term commitment "to honor and love" this research niche and a long-term commitment to maintain that love as best you can? While it is true that an arranged marriage can work—witness the scores of graduate students who simply adopt an advisor's research niche in order to expedite a dissertation only to find themselves continuing the focus throughout a successful career—it is preferable to find a niche that tugs at your heart.

Although we advocate thoughtfully selecting an area of scholarly focus, and then sticking with it during the pre-tenure years, there are at least two caveats. First, many genuine scholars reading this guide are fully capable of sustaining more than one stream of scholarly work simultaneously. These academics are bright, motivated, brimming with curiosity and endowed with seemingly boundless energy. The rest of us mere mortals admire their capacity for intellectual multitasking while humbly recognizing that we could not so gracefully manage diverging scholarly foci. Second, there will be times in the careers of scholars when it becomes clear that an existing area of inquiry has run its course; the writer discovers that, for quite some time, he or she has been driving on cruise control in a scholarly cul-de-sac. In these instances, it may be better to change course than to languish in an area that offers no opportunity for further progress. Finally, as years go by, it is healthy to maintain openness to fresh paradigms, novel research strategies, and even entirely new areas of scholarship. At times, selecting a new writing niche is a matter of following your heart and adapting to changing times. Stubbornly clinging to a stream of scholarship when it is clear that genuine emotional connection and excitement have dried up is one form of intellectual suicide. Keep your passion alive.

4   Take Control of Your Day

Here is a guarantee: Unless you grab firm control of every minute in your day, week, and semester, your writing will be occasional, disjointed, and marginally productive. Prolific academics create writing time where none exists and then carefully protect it from intrusion. As a scholar, time may be your most precious resource; it must be dogmatically protected and punctiliously respected.

One of the most common refrains from the chorus of new faculty goes something like this: "I'd love to get more writing done, if only I had some time to do it!" Many of us can empathize with this experience. Academe is often frantic-paced—especially for the early-career professor. But it is also true that too many academics fall prey to the syndrome of *professorial drift*; we float through our days without establishing clear schedules, setting firm boundaries, or thoughtfully prioritizing daily activities. In order to become prolific—something that will require writing each day—it is imperative that you turn off the autopilot and grab the controls of daily planning with a dogged determination.

In our own consultations with busy new faculty members—often frustrated writers—we recommend a behavioral exercise designed to enhance insight and awareness about time allocation. Given the presumed constant of a 24-hour day, where does each of those precious 1440 minutes go? For a period of one week—including the weekend—keep a log of how you spend each 15-minute segment. Be specific. Rather than write "in office" or "working on administrative tasks" for a one-hour period between classes, specify exactly what you did. Be just as concrete with your description of evening and weekend hours.

After diligently time-tracking for even one day, academics are often surprised and chagrined to realize how much of their discretionary time is offered up to the gods of distraction and inefficiency. Unnecessary, and often redundant, activities (e.g., browsing the Web, checking for new e-mail messages, chatting with colleagues, watching television) often occupy a prominent place in the daily log. Reflect soberly on your daily time allocation. Even if two hours of time each workday, and probably more on the weekend, are currently not well spent, think of the increase in writing time this would mean. What could you accomplish with an additional 15 hours of time to engage in scholarship each week?

Let's be clear that we are not advocating writing at the expense of other activities essential to your identity as professor, family member, and human being. To the contrary, we believe that you will be a more focused and effective writer if you are teaching effectively, taking care of yourself, nurturing important relationships, and engaging the world recreationally. Stories of academics neglecting their families or their own personal health abound; such behavior will surely be fodder for regret later on. Instead, we advocate that you honestly consider how you currently spend your discretionary time each day. On a typical day at work, how much time is devoted to nonessential tasks? In the evening, is there an hour or two—if you have children, perhaps after they have gone to bed—when you can turn on the laptop and write?

As you soberly consider your current approach to allocating the 1440 minutes you are blessed with each day, ask yourself if some of those minutes could be diverted toward scholarship simply by seeking greater efficiency. Can you make fewer trips to the store, across campus, or even down the hall of your building merely by planning more carefully? Make piles of things to mail, faxes to send, or lists of material to find in the library; rather than attend to each task independently, consolidate these into a single trip. If you must attend a large meeting or presentation that you know is certain to send you into a state of deep sleep, take along an article draft to proofread or a book to skim. If you are advising students regarding course or program requirements, aim to schedule a single group session with all of your advisees rather than separate appointments for each. You get the idea; seek parsimony and efficiency in all that you do.

When you discover that you can indeed carve out time for writing every day, block it prominently on your schedule and post this on your door. When time for writing arrives, close your door and lock it. Abide by the chemical principle of impermeability. Although pressures outside the door will inevitably build as you write, it is crucial that you maintain an impermeable boundary around your scheduled writing time. Physical laws suggest that outside demands will rush in to fill an open space. This is why your writing space must be sealed and vigorously protected.

Finally, experience has taught us that new academics frequently believe they do not have permission to block time for scholarship. They may assume that they cannot really control their schedules, that doors must always be open to students, or that they must say yes to every new invitation to join a committee or each new assignment from a department chair or dean. By and large, these assumptions are incorrect. The truth is that if you do not take control of your schedule, neither will anybody else, and you will continue to drift through the crucial early years in academe without launching yourself as a productive scholar. If nobody in your department has yet done this for you, then allow us to have the honor: We give you permission to evaluate your time allocation, streamline your duties, block chunks of time for writing each week, shut your office door, and then follow through dogmatically.

5   WRITE EVERY DAY

Prolific scholars write every day or almost every day. Daily writing is the only way for new academics to make writing a well honed habit. Those of us who engage in distance running can relate to runners' stories of discomfort, agitation, and unrest on those rare days when they cannot manage to squeeze in a good run. For these athletes, the body—and specifically the brain—have become acclimated to, and perhaps more than a little dependent upon, a daily infusion of the endorphins that accompany vigorous exercise. When committed writers establish a daily writing regimen and begin to enjoy both the experience and outcomes associated with this routine, they are equally likely to discover a sense of urgency about getting back on track.

One of the common objections to daily writing voiced by new faculty goes something like this: "Taking time for writing every day would mean taking time away from my teaching, family, or other important obligations." We understand this concern. Yet we believe it belies an erroneous assumption about the place and importance of scholarship in the academic's life. This perspective assumes that writing is something to get to when you can, only after other demands have been addressed and activities completed. From this perspective, time for scholarship gets short shrift. But if making time to write each day received the same priority as sleeping, exercising, teaching, and spending time with a partner or children, then, one's perspective would quickly change. It makes no more sense to blame a brief writing block for compromising quality of life than it does to blame preparing for class or helping children with homework. New writers must undergo a pervasive shift in their core belief about academic writing; they must transition from "*either* life or writing" to "*both* writing and life."

Why write everyday? Don't scholars need long and uninterrupted blocks of writing time to make any real progress? Wouldn't an hour be insufficient, just enough time to get you frustrated but not enough to get you on your way? Although it is certainly the case that longer stretches of writing are preferred and infinitely more likely to lead to substantial output than abbreviated time slots (for reinforcement of this idea, see the next section), it is also true that daily writing—even if opportunities are relatively brief some days—is essential. Knowing you will devote some time to writing on your current project each day keeps you close to the material and more likely to find seamless transitions back to writing; frequent exposure breeds familiarity and keeps interest fresh.

On those days when you do not stay home to write for six hours or more, or when you cannot close your office door for a few hours, can you at least arrange a full hour to get back to your project? Remember, there are often many tasks associated with producing an article or working on a book chapter that are best described as mundane or administrative. Use a scheduled hour to jot down insights, do some data analysis, collect or compile references, read an important source, proofread the existing manuscript, consult with an expert on a challenging aspect of your work, address formatting and stylistic issues, or outline the next major section to be tackled. Using this time well positions you to hit the ground running when your next substantial writing block rolls around.

Is there anything catastrophic about missing a day or two of writing? No. As the advertising slogan of one leading insurance company often reminds us, *life comes at you fast*. Be flexible enough to bend when things hit the fan, when you or a loved one becomes ill, or when you genuinely need to "stand down" for a day of rest or a week of vacation. But all things considered, it is in your best interest to make writing a daily habit. The more days elapsed without writing, the more anxious you may become, which is counterproductive, and the farther you will feel from the nexus of key ideas and purposeful momentum. Your writing apparatus, like many mechanisms, will typically work best when frequently exercised.

6   Schedule Writing Blocks

It is no surprise that famous novelists such as Stephen King and Tom Clancy abide by ironclad daily writing schedules, often starting early in the morning and extending until at least early afternoon. In order to make genuine headway on a novel or a scholarly article, there is simply no substitute for an extended and uninterrupted block of time. For an academic striving to complete a demanding piece of writing, a full or half-day sequestered at home or in one's office can feel like a profound gift. It is. We suggest that writing blocks—something we urge you to schedule at least two or three times per week—must be honored as sacred and used for maximal gain. You owe this to yourself, your students, and your institution.

Earlier in this guide, we encouraged you to be adamant about scheduling the equivalent of two full days (in various full- or half-day combinations) for uninterrupted writing. Unless you are on vacation, enjoying a sabbatical, or have a job we would both envy, it may be unrealistic to expect more writing time while striving for excellence in teaching and mentoring, and contributing service to your university. Of course, depending on your situation, you might count on additional blocks on the weekends. It goes without saying that the beauty of extended writing periods is the opportunity to wade in, become fully immersed in the project, and push ahead for significant progress before having to resurface and rejoin the external world.

Remember that the opportunity to engage in extended writing jags is a luxury and having this privilege extended, and perhaps even increased, may hinge on your ability to "show them the money." You know what "the money" is—conference papers, articles, grants, books, and so forth. Give power-holders cause to reinforce your writing behavior with even more discretionary time. Keep this in mind: If the boon of writing blocks is the promise of unmitigated focus and progress, then the bane is the sometimes difficult requirement to forgo distractions, sustain focus, and overcome fatigue. Sometimes even mundane human requirements can pose vexing dilemmas. One of us occupies the campus office farthest from the nearest lavatory in an exceptionally long building. Not only does a simple trip to the bathroom require an eighth-of-a-mile journey, it necessitates passing the offices of each colleague and being exposed to the lurking dangers of extended social interactions. When a request to install a portable toilet in the office was shot down by both the maintenance and health departments, this author learned that precious writing blocks were best safeguarded by quietly slipping out of the building and over to a nearby athletic facility to use the lavatory—a time-consuming and inelegant solution for an avid writer who is also a compulsive coffee drinker. It is not enough to block out writing time; you must ardently protect it.

How should you approach a half- or full-day writing session? Is it best to plan your time carefully, or preferable to just wade right in? The answers to these questions hinge to a large extent on your predilections and the nature of the project(s) with which you are engaged. Here are two good rules of thumb: (1) in general, it is better to organize your time in advance; and (2) the longer the writing block, the more important advanced planning becomes. If you are someone who works best with a schedule and a plan—perhaps including "to do" lists allowing you to check off completed tasks as you go—then by all means create a plan for each writing block. In addition to being introverted, many successful academics also lean in the direction of obsessive-compulsive behavior. Without lists and plans they may become paralyzed. Other academics eschew detailed session planning in favor of a broad mental framework, while still others prefer to simply let the spirit guide them as it were. In the end, your ability to get the writing done will serve as definitive evidence of the efficacy of your approach.

There is a final facet of writing blocks to thoughtfully consider. This is the issue of what we refer to as *writing transitions*, or the period of time you require to both "warm-up" to the task and subsequently "cool down" as your writing retreat draws to a close. For most of us, the warm-up phase is generally less problematic. You might feel inclined to reserve a few minutes after the door is closed (and locked), after the computer is turned on, and after your materials are arrayed before you to make a plan for the hours you will spend writing, to refresh yourself with the point at which you discontinued the writing last time, and perhaps to review key points in your working draft.

While the start-up transition is likely to be ripe with promise and positive expectation, the wind-down or wrap-up phase can carry a wider range of emotional reactions and irrational thoughts. It is quite common to feel frustrated when writing has been sluggish or lackluster. At times you may be appalled by what could only be a malevolent time warp; you wonder where all your time went. It is easy to engage in self-deprecation on those days when the right words are hard to find. And conversely, writing time often seems to expire at the penultimate moment—just when you are on a proverbial roll and the way through to completing your project has finally become clear. Anticipate the need for a cool-down period. Before packing up your material and saving your files, jot down some notes to assist you when you again start in, lean back and skim your work, and, on those days when the writing has gone well, savor the post-writing euphoria that accompanies genuine productivity. After all, you've earned it!

7   CAPTURE TIME BY WRITING IN THE "GAPS"

Now that you have taken control of your day, constructed a daily writing schedule, and carved out inviolable writing blocks several times each week, here is one more secret to prolific academic writing: Be ready to write in the gaps. In the lexicon of productive academics, gaps are those spaces or in-between moments—often occurring several times a day and hundreds of times a year—in which you suddenly find yourself with a free hour after a meeting is canceled, waiting in a long line, or otherwise maintaining a holding pattern until your next scheduled activity. Gaps are sometimes apparent when looking ahead at your daily planner. At other times, they are utterly unanticipated. On these occasions, they can have the feel of an unexpected opportunity or a delightful gift. Whether they arrive unbidden or in predictable fashion, we encourage you to be ready for gaps. Don't wait for the "perfect" time to write, as much can be done in the meantime during those in-between moments. Grab time! One of us found ourselves recently sharing this advice with a faculty member who enjoys a considerable research allocation of 25 percent of his time. Unfortunately, he has often waited until the summer months to write, thereby artificially truncating both the consistency and volume of his writing.

Although many reading this guide will insist that they can only make important progress on a project if sequestered away for a long writing block, we have discovered that some of the more creative elements of scholarly writing (e.g., reflecting on your topic, crafting the outline of a future article, trouble-shooting a research design) as well as many of the more mundane elements (e.g., editing a draft, checking references, making notes on or from other sources, writing an abstract) lend themselves perfectly to short bursts of activity. Of course, effectively writing in the gaps requires two important ingredients: (1) you must be deliberate and intentional about preparing for gap time; and (2) when the gaps arise, you must follow through and focus on your scholarship to the exclusion of competing options (e.g., naps, Web surfing, magazine reading, spontaneous chats). The first ingredient can easily be achieved by taking scholarly tools along with you during the day. If your briefcase contains some articles you need to read and distill, or drafts of your latest work to edit, you will be prepared to make the most of free time. If you anticipate longer gaps, take along a laptop and more of the necessary material you'll need to be productive.

In our experience, extra writing time can be captured where none existed simply by being prepared to do some work in such circumstances as sitting in a doctor's office waiting for an appointment, standing in line at the Department of Motor Vehicles, sitting in your office during a half-hour stretch between classes or meetings, during down-time at a convention, waiting for repairs to be completed on your car, for a child's soccer practice to end, or even standing around in your kitchen while pasta cooks. And don't forget unexpected delays and idle time spent in trains, planes, and automobiles and on platforms. On recent trips to New York via train and San Francisco via airplane, we were both able to plug in our laptops and enjoy extended hours of delightful productivity punctuated by inspiring landscapes and garnished with hot beverages. As another example, a child's indoor track meet typically involves about three hours of parental waiting. While being present to support kids is a paramount commitment, the 170 minutes of waiting is often an ideal opportunity for attending to various writing tasks. You get the idea. Productive academics do not complain that they can only work at their desk or at home; instead, they capture additional writing time by "writing in" life's gaps—pun intended!

Here is a fascinating phenomenon: The more you write, and the more you begin to enjoy writing, the more likely you will be to naturally turn your attention to scholarship when opportunities present themselves. Call this scholarly inertia. When writing—and all the tasks associated with the scholarly enterprise—become so thoroughly integrated into life that you naturally seek opportunities to continue the process in-between larger writing blocks, you will have turned a corner; for prolific scholars, writing in the gaps makes the difference in promoting high productivity.

As you might suspect, we close this discussion with a caveat and a friendly warning. Although writing in the gaps is a wonderful way to exponentially increase productivity, be careful. Make sure you guard against what we call *academic nerdism*. We define nerdism as a tendency to become so preoccupied with using every available minute for writing that one becomes either distressed (e.g., anxious, depressed, sleep deprived) or dysfunctional (e.g., fails to meet important obligations, ignores loved ones, allows relationships to suffer, misses out on other joys and pleasures in life). For academics that already suffer from obsessive tendencies, writing in the gaps can take on a compulsive character fueled by anxiety. In this case, enjoyment will almost certainly be diminished. Keep writing but keep it in perspective.

8   STAY HOME (OR LOCKED IN A TOWER)

Successful writers learn early on that the most productive writing often occurs when sequestered away in the familiar comfort of home, the sanctuary of a hotel room during an otherwise busy conference, in the quiet recesses of a comfortable basement, an anonymous library cubical, or a secluded weekend cabin. Each of these writing locations shares one important feature in common: It is far from your office and its unceasing stream of interruptions and distractions. As realtors are fond of saying, *location is everything*. To write prolifically, it is often imperative to write away from campus.

During the regular workweek, we highly recommend that you firmly limit your teaching and meeting obligations to no more than three days per week. Schedule meetings on your teaching days and block the other two days for writing. Many reading this advice will say, "but I'm too busy, I can't afford to block out two full days." To this, we respond, if you're tenure-earning at a research institution, you can't afford not to. Once your teaching schedule is set for the semester—and we recommend that you be assertive about influencing decisions regarding when your classes are scheduled—select two days or four half-days and block them out with permanent marker for the entire semester. Believe it or not, department leaders, colleagues, and students will quickly acclimate to this schedule and learn to request meetings on the days you're available.

An outrageously prolific scholar at Vanderbilt University, a former department chair, advised junior professors about how to develop their scholarship and increase their productivity. The young colleagues who received their chair's counsel were urged to stay home and write at least twice weekly, consolidating meetings on days they were in the office. His sage advice went something like this:

> You can only be productive if you work. It sounds simple, but you have to get to the workbench every day. You can't say, "I'm going to work on my article on Monday or Friday." This is not going to help. You've got to be really specific, diligent, and aggressive about setting a schedule for your scholarship and sticking to it. You have to work on your scholarship, and if you don't allot the time to do it, it's not going to automatically occur.

Although we titled this section "Stay Home," we recognize that home will not be conducive to productivity for all new academics. Some of us have children at home, some of us have active roommates, and still others may find home so chock full of tempting distractions that we can't seem to bear down and attend exclusively to the task at hand. If any of this rings true, then it is imperative for you to find an alternative writing hide-away—a place with no distracting trappings, a place you can associate exclusively with writing. Call this your local writing address. It may be a vacant office across campus, a friend's spare room, or a cubicle in the library. At our institutions (the University of South Florida and the U.S. Naval Academy), faculty can easily reserve very small—closet-sized—rooms for the semester or year. These rooms feature four bare walls, a desk, a chair, outlets for your computer, and a solid door with a reliable lock. Once the door to such a monastic chamber is closed, there is very little to do but write! Of course, once you are ensconced at your local writing address, you will need to avoid answering the door, responding to phone calls or checking e-mail— allowing such distractions undermines the very reason for securing a writing space.

Here is another recommendation for new academics: When you are afforded longer stretches of time away from your department, consider using some of this for writing. You will find yourself traveling to a convention or a speaking engagement, as well as taking holidays and vacations, so why not bring along your laptop and writing files? Both of us have enjoyed writing articles, books, and proposals on jaunts around the world as well as in beach condos. Spring and summer breaks offer ideal times for achieving major progress on writing projects. In these instances, create a writing schedule *before* departing for a vacation or a conference: Discipline yourself to steal moments or even hours while away to get some important work done. Even at crowded conventions or on long travel days, "down time" can occur as an unexpected surprise.

We refer to those delightful—and all too rare—occasions when you can actually plan time away exclusively for the purpose of scholarly work as *writing vacations*. Plan and utilize your time for maximum effect. To start, we recommend that you develop a checklist. That way you will be sure to have all of the papers and sources you need, as well as all of that "fussy" equipment for your laptop that makes or breaks productivity. External disk drives, external keyboards, power cables, and thumbdrives are just a few examples. It's a good idea to save your entire set of files on your thumbdrive or on a CD ROM, should you want to access files unexpectedly. Writing can be organic and unpredictable, sending you to ideas recorded elsewhere in your research, teaching, and service files. As another pointer, if you are noise sensitive, book your room away from the elevator and other high-traffic areas. And by all means, if you are fortunate enough to have a writing vacation in a lovely area, take time for walks, swims, or bike rides as a way of refreshing and refocusing in the midst of the work.

Finding the right balance of work and rejuvenation will be the key to making your writing vacation a success. Although writing is usually a solo endeavor, there are times when a writing vacation can incorporate a coauthor or at least another author. Near the end of graduate school, one of us spent an entire week at a mountain cabin with a best friend. Not only did both of us successfully write the majority of our dissertation literature reviews over the course of the week, we went on long runs each day, enjoyed cooking to break the long hours of monotony, and became closer friends along the way.

Here's the key: When you write in long jags, stay away. Hide. Do not make yourself available by phone, except for urgent messages. One of us received an enticing job offer while on a one-week writing holiday. Although welcomed news that inspired greater productivity, it was important to stay the course and keep working. Even good news can wait until after your work is done. The rule of thumb here is to avoid distractions and even the appearance of inviting these. And don't worry what anyone thinks of your well-timed absences—as long as you're productive and have something to show for your time. It is a good idea to let someone, perhaps your department chair or office secretary, know where you are while away.

An essential lesson born of personal experience is that prolific writers get more time for writing. Smart institutional leaders often grant their most productive scholars greater degrees of freedom when it comes to independence and time away to write. They may more easily overlook your absence at nonessential faculty meetings, endorse your plan to work away from the office routinely, and protect you from assignment to institution-wide committees. Sometimes this is deliberate, at other times it is unconscious, but institutional leaders are simply inclined to reward professors who come through with evidence of productivity. Seasoned scholars are usually good at navigating administration and negotiating rewards for their efforts, such as course releases, graduate assistantship, and office space. Prolific scholars usually leave institutions that fail to reward productivity or afford them ample time for writing.

When you get a major contract for a book or grant, or will be undertaking a time-consuming writing project, see what, if anything, administrators can do to support you. And remember: Each year is a new slate in terms of one's productivity. A department chair has been known to say to his faculty that it didn't matter how much they had produced the previous year, what mattered was "What have you done for me lately"? This sent a powerful message to the group—no professor has laurels to rest upon, unless he or she is retired.

Strive for outstanding productivity and appreciate the fact that this will only make your administrator and institution look good. Knowing this should empower you to selfishly guard precious writing time without feeling guilty. But in all cases remain collegial.

2

BECOME DOGMATICALLY DISCIPLINED AND SET FIRM BOUNDARIES

After a decision to write is crystallized, it is time to establish several ironclad policies regarding the fierce protection of your writing space. It is time to become a disciplined writer. Carefully weigh the demands of service and teaching on your time and try to focus on responsibilities that promote your development as an academic writer. Being an overly accommodating colleague will only "reward" you with more and more nonresearch commitments. Monitor the equity in faculty load distribution at your institution as a way of ensuring fairness in work allocation. It is also imperative that you pursue your own writing pace; be a good mentor and colleague, but don't get bogged down by underfunctioning or distracting colleagues. It is possible to be dogmatically protective of your writing boundaries while simultaneously being a valued colleague.

9 TAKE VOWS OF DISCIPLINE AND DELAYED GRATIFICATION

Scott Peck (1978) struck a powerful chord in the opening line to his bestseller *The Road Less Traveled* with the words, "Life is difficult." The writing life is also difficult. If you want to be a prolific writer, be prepared to sacrifice and endure some inevitable pain. On the surface, this sounds easy enough, but remember, human beings are programmed to avoid pain at all costs; sometimes, pushing through discomfort and boredom will require doing battle with powerful urges to sidestep, postpone, or quit your project altogether. Wading through hours of tedious literature-reviewing and data analysis, and dedicating oneself to working especially when the tasks are formidable or unpleasant, is the very soul of the disciplined writing life. Once a writing schedule is established, stick to it. In no other area of your professorial life are dogmatism and rigidity so essential and likely to pay tangible dividends.

We know, we're making it sound like you need to become a monk or nun in order to succeed in the academy, but the reality is that a monastic frame of mind during the hours you allocate to writing can be a virtue. Like monks and nuns, productive writers seek sanctuaries to reflect, take vows of discipline, and delay gratification. Of course, sabbaticals offer the chance to become more thoroughly immersed in the austere mindset of the academic monastic. The most dogmatically self-disciplined scholars are often prolific writers. When you carefully observe them you will notice that they have clear, even firm, boundaries, know how to delegate tasks, and write (almost) everyday—few are procrastinators, at least not chronically.

Prolific scholars tend to have other attributes in common. These include vision, focus, optimism, and emotional resilience. Difficult personal problems and workplace conflicts are overcome more readily because these people are so focused on their writing goals and maintain perspective on what matters to them. If the work environment is not conducive to writing, they simply stay at home even more than usual to work. Every new day is rife with choices. Without a doubt, prolific writing is a choice, not merely a choice to write but a simultaneous choice to not engage in alternative behaviors that tend to impede writing. On the spectrum of gratification, writing seldom offers anything immediate—beyond some intrinsic satisfaction with making progress or getting more words down on the page. Indeed, prolific writing is typically a prime example of delayed gratification. Can you go long periods exerting diligent effort for tangible rewards that are both distant and unpredictable? Although most graduate students and junior faculty reading this guide have already shown their mettle when it comes to delayed gratification, all of us are vulnerable to running off course.

Let's be clear that delayed gratification does not mean ignoring opportunities to celebrate important milestones, or brushing aside one's self-care, or neglecting important relationships. Medical attention, physical activity, and other practices that promote good health and well-being are "musts." Prolific scholars tend to have obsessive-compulsive work habits; some adhere to regular exercise routines, but the aging process combined with scheduling demands can conspire to take over. These pose great challenges for all academics. It is also important to note that self-discipline and an unflinching commitment to write must never trump excellent teaching or availability to students. Further, it is a miscarriage of responsibility to leave all service demands in your department to tenure-earning faculty if you yourself hold tenure. The balanced scholar exhibits stringent commitment to scholarship in the context of full membership in the academy.

The daily habits of tenure-earning faculty make a big difference in the long haul—eating at the computer instead of at the dinner table or in front of the TV, for example, and putting aside favorite shows and pleasure reading are ways of "banking" time. As other examples, long trips to visit family and friends should get replaced with short ones, unless you can do your writing during your stay. Just like penny-saving, small efforts do add up. The more productively you use your time, and the more sacrifices you make—small, not just big—the greater the results.

Start banking today.

10   "JUST SAY NO" TO COMPETING DEMANDS

School leaders, parents, and even presidents have counseled us to "just say no" when it is important to. Most of us intuit that saying "no" sometimes can be healthy and critical to insuring maximal performance. Yet how many of us reluctantly say "yes" time and time again? And after becoming overcommitted, how many of us complain relentlessly, all the while feeling like a martyr? We go through all of that, when one little word—two little letters, even!—could have freed us from obligation: No. Sorry, no. Darn it, no way, I can't. Or, the more daring: Not only no, but hell no! That's what your inner voice was bellowing as your tenure-earning mouth uttered, "Yes, I'd love to assume your student advising load while you take sabbatical next semester," or "Okay, I'll attend weekly three-hour faculty senate meetings all year."

There are myriad reasons why otherwise high-functioning college professors struggle with saying "no." Some of us exhibit symptoms of self-doubt or shame when compelled to set limits and say no—particularly when authority figures are involved. This syndrome has been termed "the disease to please." Lacking confidence as professionals, we may naively assume that senior colleagues know best and will always have our interests at heart. Sometimes, new faculty erroneously assume that saying yes to every request will help them win tenure and promotion, when in fact good teaching and stellar scholarship are the primary criteria for tenure. Life-skills coaches warn that saying yes when you need or want to say no causes burnout and other negative health outcomes. Keep in mind that we do the people making the request a disservice and certainly ourselves by constantly saying yes.

Let's face it, once you decide to write, nearly everything in your life will conspire to derail you. Because academics—especially educators—are naturally curious, service-oriented, and prone to enjoy work with students and colleagues, opportunities for engaging in the academic milieu are nearly endless. Mail, e-mail, phone calls, and interesting reading can also become deeply alluring when writing time rolls around. Turn off the "interruptions" and shut them out. Here is the paradox: As your reputation grows, so will the volume of requests, invitations, and flat-out demands on your time. The more productive you become, the more dogmatic you will have to be in your determination to set boundaries around your writing time. Become adept at separating priorities from the distractions.

Or course, you cannot and should not say no to every request. Prolific academics quickly learn to separate demands that are reasonable from those that are not. It's not always easy to make this determination, especially in the face of an unexpected request. Try this technique: As someone asks you to do something, take a deep breath. Don't agree immediately. Give yourself time to decide. If you know you want to say no and just can't seem to politely decline on the spot, just say you will get back to them. Avoid feeling pressure and saying yes only to regret it later on. To hone your skill in this area, observe how seasoned professionals respond to impromptu requests; notice how smoothly they can refuse requests without tripping over their words, justifying themselves, or wallowing in anguish. They simplify by depersonalizing the situation and offering the same explanation to everyone they decline. Here are some effective examples: "That's a great idea and I wish you well with it." "I'm sorry but I already have too much on my plate right now to be of any service." "Having children to take care of at home makes it difficult for me to accept any more responsibility at this time." And, "I really don't have the expertise or the interest in that area, but here are some names you might consider." Here is one colleague's creative response we term the Before Tenure (BT)/After Tenure (AT) technique. Our colleague often applied it with a friendly flare: "Listen, you can definitely count on me to do that AT. In the meantime, I'm BT and must regrettably say no." Others, including the dean, soon warmed up to her, despite the rejections, and even adopted her lingo. You will seldom find an academic administrator who is not sensitive to this issue.

As a beginning professor, you may feel compelled to succumb to various pressures applied by senior faculty. We know people who, from their first week on the job, delayed their own writing productivity by providing manuscript reviews for their new colleagues or acquiescing to excessive committee assignments. Set a clear precedent early on that protects your writing time. Do you tend to accommodate the wishes of department chairs and anyone else who smacks of authority to you? If you see the department chair as your "boss" or the tenure review committee as an all-powerful group never to be defied, you may have difficulty acting with the autonomy that should characterize a college professor. Freedom is, in a word, the soul of the academy; academic freedom is what draws many of us to the professoriate. You are your own "boss" now—chairs are your colleagues, just as senior faculty are, and while they do have an evaluative role, you are in charge of and ultimately accountable for your own academic career and writing life.

Intelligently filter any "unreasonable" requests by senior faculty and administrators. If you're being asked to do something that truly is unreasonable, and have no choice but to rise to the occasion, start negotiating. Tenure-earning faculty get asked to teach new courses with little notice and thus preparation time, to teach out-of-discipline, to chair the recruiting efforts for their programs, and to head up the accreditation process for their college or department, among other things. When someone asks you to do something that could jeopardize your advancement, seriously consider whether there is any way you can benefit: Compromise in a way that will support your writing efforts. However, if upon declining you experience penalty, investigate your faculty rights and assert them with respect to your assigned duties. Learn from politically savvy faculty who know how to gain from compromises. Common bargaining chips include release time from a course, graduate assistance, extra clerical support, and summer salary. Finagle but stay focused on your writing!

When all is said and done, the more dogmatically disciplined you are about your writing agenda, the more others will naturally respect your firm boundaries. Come across as confident, not overly accommodating or unable to say no to competing demands.

Be your own best friend.

11   REBUKE THE DEMONS OF SERVICE

It's true that service to institution and profession constitute one leg of the traditional academic stool, but do not kid yourself—teaching and scholarship are what count most at promotion and tenure junctures, and, even then, scholarship reigns supreme. No matter what your research university says, prolific scholars are more likely to be promoted than great teachers, active committee members, and committed service volunteers. New professors must ask the question, "How might this commitment serve both the institution and my own scholarly goals; how will it help me get tenured?" in response to each new request to serve an organization in some capacity. Examples include joining a committee, assuming leadership in a professional association, organizing conference symposia, preparing student orientations, and agreeing to serve on thesis and dissertation committees.

Service is important and some degree of service is nonnegotiable, but service can easily become a drain on your scholarly resources. Without careful management, service can become the enemy of writing productivity, stability, and routine. In our experience, junior faculty frequently make the mistake of demonstrating porous boundaries to department chairs or other senior faculty. Afraid to disappoint and laboring under the illusion that service and scholarship are coequal at promotion and tenure junctures, they take on Herculean service loads while their writing slowly falters and productivity fades.

Since you will definitely be doing some service, think smart. There is an implicit hierarchical value attached to most forms of service—service within your college or university is generally valued less than service to your profession. While serving on your department's various faculty committees (e.g., accreditation, admissions, recruitment) may have internal value, and although each of us owes some allegiance to our departments and institutions, the rewards can be lean, especially come the tenure decision. The further you venture from "home," then, the better: That goes for activity on your campus outside your department and certainly for service within your field. High-energy, focused, tenure-earning faculty usually join editorial boards of journals and other publishing presses, review for the journals, associations, and funding agencies in which they seek publication or sponsorship, and assume a leadership role within their favorite professional association. Keep a careful record and supporting evidence of all such activity. It is probably apparent that key service roles within your discipline can actually facilitate your scholarly output. For example, reviewing manuscripts and serving on the program committee for your field's premier conference are forms of service likely to bring you—and your work—to the attention of important colleagues and potential collaborators.

Develop your own policy or practice as to how you will approach service each semester and year. Someone we know who was recently tenured recommends keeping active with at least one service commitment to your department, college, university, and field. He looks for the most visible committees to serve on at his campus that demand the least amount of work, and gave, as examples, publication, library, and senate committees. Ask around and see what tips your colleagues can offer you. Of course, the relative value and workload for all such committees vary from one institution to the next and from year to year. No doubt, as a tenure-track faculty member you likely will be haunted by the demons of service. Although it is vital that you serve your campus and your profession, be selective: To the extent possible, your service commitments should enhance your writing productivity and overall scholarship. As an example, one of us routinely served on a research award committee and on a summer faculty grant committee; these committees offered an insider's view to the work of highly prolific scholars on campus, and the committee work was generally limited to a short period during the academic year. The strategies you bring to selecting your service involvement and commitments can make a world of difference to your success as a scholar.

12 CONNECT YOUR WRITING TO TEACHING AND SERVICE

Prolific scholars turn the teaching/research/service requirement for faculty excellence into a "package deal." Outstanding professors have a tendency to integrate these essential components of faculty performance by seeking areas of overlap. The greater the match between teaching, service, and scholarship, the more economical and elegant your work will become.

Many professors turn the demands of teaching and service into "fodder" for research. In fact, these holistic thinkers have difficulty viewing one major activity in isolation from another; they naturally gravitate toward making creative connections among seemingly disparate areas. The umbrella term "scholarship" is most fitting for these visionary individuals. They have developed overarching themes that bind and connect research to teaching and service. For example, new professors who use their classroom teaching as the basis for scholarly inquiry will find a fundamental connection, as will those who write with the students they teach or supervise and those who turn major service commitments into research projects (e.g., evaluating institutional outcomes as a member of the institution's assessment committee). Service demands in faculty and policy development, program accreditation and renewal, and institutional and cultural change all make potentially ripe topics for inquiry.

You've probably noticed that scholarship is sometimes used to refer to research only and sometimes it is extended to teaching and service. In his groundbreaking classic *Scholarship Reconsidered: Priorities of the Professoriate*, Ernest Boyer (1990) presented a case for the latter scenario. He recognized that faculty reward systems have yet to match the wide range of academic functions that define our work as professors and that cause us to feel "caught between competing obligations" (p. 1). He defined scholarship broadly in an effort to capture the complete gambit of our work. The scholarship of discovery—that is research—is too restrictive a view of scholarship, Boyer argued, so he added the scholarships of integration, application, and teaching.

For example, many faculty members in the field of education seek connectedness between their research and teaching; teaching may take on the mantel of serious intellectual endeavor. It is not just a forum for sharing knowledge and teaching skills but a context in which our developmental needs as scholars can be met. Perhaps due to Boyer's influence, many colleges and universities now require tenure-seeking faculty to list separately publications that arise from their teaching context. If this modest change tells us anything, it is that the scholarly value placed on teaching, and on the teacher as scholar, has finally snagged the recognition of administrators of particular disciplines.

Writing can be facilitated when you consciously seek to "marry" your research and teaching. A few examples of topics that have come to fruition through our teaching are student engagement, cohort mentoring, theory-practice relations, web-enhanced instruction, administrator preparation, pre-service teacher empowerment, cultural identity, and disabilities awareness.

Also, seek creative ways to integrate your scholarship into your major service commitments. This will probably be harder to accomplish than integrating teaching and scholar-ship, in which pedagogical experiments can be developed and "data" generated through such means as interviews and sur-veys. Nonetheless, even with your service commitments you can produce academic writing on topics relevant to your aca-demic interests and seek publication of the results. We man-aged to do some of this while tenure-earning, although the "light bulb" would usually go off only after we were immersed in the work at hand. As an example, we turned service on a college's research council into a published article on the vision of differentiated staffing for colleges of educa-tion; for this purpose, data were collected from faculty nationwide after having carefully documented the varied responses of the on-site committee participants. As another example, after having coordinated an extramural mentoring program for new scholars for the American Educational Research Association, a leading national conference, one of us surveyed the participating mentoring parties. The research that featured an innovative form of academic mentoring appeared in an international journal. In another instance, one of us collected outcome data that emerged while coordinat-ing a university-wide, campus-led mentoring initiative for undergraduate students engaged in research with faculty. Finally, one of us became intrigued by the process of screen-ing professionals for personal character and psychological fitness while serving on a state Board of Bar Examiners. By extrapolating from law to the discipline of psychology, three peer-reviewed articles were published on the topic.

The artificial lines many faculty seem to draw in the sand sep-arating research from teaching and service are limiting. Here is the bottom line: Productive faculty members become adept at producing scholarship wherever they are; that is, within their service, teaching, and institutional context, they find elegant and economical strategies for researching and writing. They see the potential for "inquiry" just about anywhere. Orchestrate research activity in the taken-for-granted spaces of your own classrooms and meeting rooms, and write about what you have learned.

13   AVOID THE FACTORY MENTALITY AND LUNCH CROWD

Every academic unit has a unique working style and set of values. If you work with committed, serious scholars and supportive staff, you will probably find that collegial distractions are kept to a minimum. However, if you work with colleagues who are unproductive procrastinators or insecure competitors, you may find yourself in an uncomfortable situation. A productive, focused newcomer may unintentionally violate implicit cultural norms and threaten the status quo, especially where unproductive senior faculty form the majority. This would not be a surprising occurrence in the academy, given that "fragmented communication" is more common than one might expect (Massy, Wilger, & Colbeck, 1994). Massey et al. interviewed approximately 300 faculty from different types of higher education institutions only to learn that faculty communication problems are widespread. Issues of autonomy, specialization, levels of civility, generational splits, and personal politics were found to be at the center of these difficulties.

As one solution, avoid the factory mentality, lunch crowd, and politicking while at the same time remaining collegial with fellow academics. You will need to find creative and steadfast ways to walk this tightrope. For one thing, set clear boundaries: Kindly but clearly communicate that you have specific goals to satisfy and within exact timeframes. Over time, you can count on at least some colleagues accepting your disciplined ways; some of them may even begin to see you as a role model. However, others may feel jealous and even threatened, especially if your work receives recognition from faculty, administrators, and the larger academic field. For another thing, circulate publishing-related information (e.g., call for proposals) to your colleagues, setting a professional tone: This action may strike a positive cord for those seeking opportunities to publish. Finally, participate as fully as possible in requisite faculty meetings and sponsored events—many of these are usually required anyway. When you take the lead in encouraging colleague's scholarly work, highlight and broadcast writing opportunities within the department, invite colleagues to participate in team projects (when appropriate), and transparently pursue your own projects, your collegiality cannot easily be questioned.

Let us define the term *factory mentality*. A factory mentality is a subtle but well-established psychosocial process in which members of a workplace labor under implicit norms about appropriate rates of productivity. Various research studies confirm that when a newcomer or an existing member of a community questions or dares to violate established norms, the remaining members often feel threatened and may take steps to pressure the discrepant member to comply with implicit norms. Depending upon the academic departmental culture, an insidious factory mentality may cause some new faculty to fear that producing more than their lowest producing senior counterparts could jeopardize their tenure. In these environments, tenure-earning professors who strive to overcome this social obstacle and write prolifically may experience both political heat and interpersonal alienation. For example, a noncompliant newcomer may be ostracized socially, given unreasonable committee loads, or be otherwise sabotaged. Consider the experience of a tenure-earning Hispanic female at a premier research institution:

> I've learned to contain my overt enthusiasm for scholarship and teaching, downplay my project involvement and publication successes, and tame my seemingly flighty ways in order to fit in. But this is not to imply that I could get away with being less than competent as a teacher and scholar, so I work doubly hard. I don't know how much any of this has to do with gender issues or the atmosphere of repression in the academy. (personal communication, December 2004)

So what to do if the factory mentality is stifling your work? First, try to ensure that your own behavior is thoroughly collegial. Nothing can exacerbate insecurity and competitiveness faster than a newcomer who comes across as secretive, withholding, and purely self-absorbed. Strike a balance between warm, sincere, and consistent collegiality and firm boundaries around your scholarly time. Finally, refuse to tolerate either subtle or overt forms of pressure to reduce your output, and confront power-holders if punished for noncompliance with normative mediocrity.

What about socializing with colleagues during the work week? It can certainly be fun, even inspiring, to go to lunch occasionally or to "brown bag" it with colleagues from inside or outside your department or college. Such sessions can provide excellent opportunities to discuss academic writing, to exchange vital information about the publishing world, or to reward yourself for productive writing. As in the case of service activities, we think it is important to be socially engaged but on your own terms. The same professor quoted previously shared that, "Because I am concerned about getting tenure and know that my department's vote will count, I join my comparatively leisurely tenured colleagues for lunch once weekly." This professor spends her remaining lunch periods and breaks honed in on writing. If you find yourself conflicted about how much socializing is expected, consider speaking with trusted administrators to seek advice and perhaps to learn about their related experiences, all in an effort to seek solutions.

We extend a cautionary note: Be an excellent colleague without giving in to norms promoting scholarly slothfulness or inactivity. If, in spite of your best efforts to balance collegiality and outrageous productivity, you find yourself alienated or otherwise sabotaged, consider moving on—you will probably have the publications to be competitive elsewhere. And here is one more secret: don't expect your department or college to reward your unusual productivity in all circumstances. Professors have often shared with us that while their annual publishing accomplishments have outrun those of their departmental colleagues, everyone in their departments is awarded the exact same annual merit raise (or none at all). Although such practices undermine the very notion of "merit," they happen. The factory mentality and the political pressure it incites can pervade administrative practice, not just faculty culture.

As we can see, where institutional and human forces embody the factory mentality, everyone is kept to the same low standards. Of course, these pressures are covert and counter to what people who act oppressively or deceptively will in fact claim to be true about their own values and work habits. Although culturally implicit, faculty will be expected to produce no more than their counterparts or they will not be recognized if their productivity is higher. You are a professor, not a lemming! Rise above thinking of your products as "widgets" or "thingamajigs," and, for goodness sake, produce scholarship at your rate, not the rate set by the herd.

14   Demand Equity in Faculty Responsibilities

Conditions within departments support or hinder fairness in the assignment of faculty duties and responsibilities. It is difficult to do the work of writing when battling excessive demands for teaching, student advising, and service. When a department chair allows new faculty to be exploited in the sense of expecting them to do more of the teaching, supervision, and committee work than is demanded of senior faculty, something is wrong. Avoid attempting to single-handedly correct a problematic departmental culture by advising more students than you should or by accepting teaching or administrative overloads. Consult your program coordinator or, if necessary, confront your department head with questions about equity. Clearly articulate your need for scholarly time and safeguards in this regard. If reasonable requests are not honored, seek support from administrative leaders in charge of overseeing tenure and promotion in your college, usually the associate dean for academic affairs or someone in a comparable position; if results are not satisfactory, consider revising expectations for your own productivity or move on to a more research-friendly institution. Remember, you are your own best guardian when it comes to screening assigned responsibilities and ensuring evenhandedness on the part of others.

In order to proceed thoughtfully in considering your assigned faculty responsibilities, consider what your assigned faculty duties look like when compared with others at the same rank and across rank within the same academic unit. Keep in mind that your dean or department chair will see your time through the lens of a matrix or calendar. Your Full-time Equivalent (FTE) must add up to 100 percent and be divided among the three major categories in which you will be evaluated—research, teaching, and service. *FTE* refers to the percentage of time a staff member works, represented as a decimal. A full-time person is 1.00, a half-time person is .50 and a quarter-time person is .25.

If you are tenure-earning, teaching and research will constitute your greatest efforts and hence percentage weights. In our experience, 40 percent or more has been allocated to each of these responsibilities, with service weighing in at 20 percent or less. Although many new faculty choose to make teaching the larger slice of their academic responsibility pie, research efforts typically require longer to produce positive results. Manuscript reviews alone can take months. Thus, for many of us, it may be wise to allocate more time to research and scholarship in the first few years of an academic career. It is easier to titrate up the amount of time you devote to teaching new courses or serving on committees *after* your scholarship is thoroughly established and publications are underway.

In much the same way that it makes sense to allocate more of your early financial portfolio to stocks, it is wise to assign more of your earlier academic time to producing scholarship. Both investments will pay larger dividends down the road than the alternatives. This advice should not be construed as license to neglect excellent teaching. We merely suggest that to the extent you can influence the process of allocation, lobby for more time to write in the first few years of your academic post. Try to be realistic about what you can accomplish within a single academic year, and what you need to accomplish to stay on track for tenure, before agreeing to an assigned load of faculty duties. Quite often, faculty experience regret after agreeing to large teaching and service loads during years that are crucial to establishing one's scholarly credentials.

The tension between teaching and scholarly time allocation can create particularly poignant conflict for the faculty member committed to both exemplary teaching and prolific writing. Bear in mind that teaching does not refer only to your courses but also to any advisements, thesis/dissertation supervisions, and directed/independent studies. Specific percentage allocations (e.g., 5 percent) can be given to duties that go beyond the teaching of courses, otherwise official credit will be lost. Because it is essential that we as faculty maintain high competence as professionals in our fields and keep abreast of the most recent developments in our special areas of scholarly interest, excellent teaching becomes more difficult without a substantial allocation of resources to scholarship. And yet, it is important to be sensitive to the fact that your official allocation of research time is likely to be less than that of more senior scholars who are prolific. Because they have track records of significant external funding or remarkable productivity, accomplished faculty members often negotiate significant research allocations.

We recognize that the pursuit of one's scholarly interests requires concentrated efforts that heavy teaching loads and other campus responsibilities strain. Do your best to keep your responsibilities outside of teaching and research to a minimum early on. Ironically, coteaching efforts can actually create a burden, costing you valuable time and energy, so give careful consideration to such initiatives. Academic departments generally lack the resources that encourage faculty collaboration and creativity in teaching assignments, and they are constrained by inflexible evaluation-and-reward structures (Massy, Wilger, & Colbeck, 1994). Different opportunities for student advisement and service activity will likely come your way, so choose wisely and within the percentage allocation you have agreed to. Doing too much advising or committee work when such activities are not fully covered in the institution's FTE matrix is a form of self-sabotage. We know a junior professor who volunteered to oversee a departmental accreditation visit, spending so much time on the organizational "trivia" associated with this kind of commitment that his tenured colleagues wondered how serious he was about his writing and tenure.

Although tenure-earning faculty are supposed to be protected from unfair expectations regarding teaching and service, this is not always the case. Theoretically, your assigned responsibilities should evolve from the tenure-earning to post-tenure, to senior academic leader phases of a career. Again, to use an investment metaphor, your allocation of investments should change as your career evolves and time to retirement draws near. But the truth is that you can't always count on department leaders to watch out for your scholarly time (or even to advise you on your assignment of responsibilities). Faculty will need to steadfastly protect their scholarly allocation and see to it that they are not being given more teaching or service than their colleagues and, savvy faculty would argue, peer institutions. You may also note that tenured faculty who obtain competitive grants and book contracts have leverage and can negotiate releases from teaching. Success often breeds opportunities for more success.

Equivalency even among new tenure-earning faculty can prove tricky to understand let alone verify. Most new hires recognize the importance of negotiating with their department chairs their percentages in advance. The politically astute will probably want to request more emphasis on teaching and scholarship early on, knowing the inordinate amount of time it takes to prepare new courses and to acclimate to a new institution. Other incoming faculty may have official administrative duties or even split appointments divided between two organizations, such as education and psychology, or between two colleges, such as science and medicine. These faculty in particular must be cautious about getting swamped with excessive administrative work or torn between competing demands, sometimes even different cultural expectations.

Remember, in the final analysis your assigned duties will go a long way toward determining how much time you can allocate to writing. Demand equity at not only the early paperwork stage but also during your tenure. Use this allocation process to direct attention to your writing commitments and, should subsequent requests come your way that fall outside your job matrix, politely decline.

15   MODEL BOUNDARIES WITHOUT NEGLECTING STUDENTS OR RETREATING

As a college professor, your first obligation is to those you serve. But there is a fine line between focus on scholarship and neglect of students and colleagues. If productive writing causes harm to your students through outright neglect, something is wrong. At the same time, if students are constantly showing up unannounced at your door you will not be able to get any writing done. You need to have posted office hours and dogmatically stick to them. Refrain from trying to serve students who really should be talking to other faculty or the administrators in your building. It is counterproductive, for example, for you to struggle with assisting the student of another dissertation chair when only that faculty expert can help anyway. By allowing yourself to become mired in every student or faculty issue that crosses the threshold of your office, you may unwittingly undermine colleagues, enable manipulative students, and ultimately sabotage your own opportunities for writing.

In our experience, excellent teaching, mentoring, collegiality, and writing need not be mutually exclusive—even in small institutions or graduate programs with large student-faculty ratios. What's the secret? Clear boundaries and good planning around daily goals. When it is time to write, lock your door, disconnect the phone, turn off e-mail, and do not compromise. When time for writing is up, open your door and engage the academic community fully. By so doing, you will be a fantastic model to your students and to less productive colleagues. In contrast to schools, government offices, and some other workplaces, we're allowed to shut our doors in the academy—our culture is unique. Our focus is not only on serving students but also on developing our professorial expertise so that we can influence our respective disciplines.

At times, faculty struggle to balance the sometimes competing roles of prolific scholar, engaged mentor, and friendly colleague. This is no easy juggling act, and even the most accomplished professors drop the ball in one or more areas. Perhaps the biggest hurdle for some is the troubling negative emotional state brought on by guilt. Those of us that are also parents often agonize over the tug to stay away and write, and the equally compelling tug to be home with children or elderly parents. Over time, prolific scholars often learn that these two essential life activities need not be mutually exclusive. Healthy parents block out time for work and adhere to those boundaries carefully. But when time comes to be home, they are thoroughly engaged and emotionally available to their children, partners, or elders. Just as children rarely experience these parents as neglectful, it is unlikely that your students or colleagues will see you as detached or uncaring—in spite of your firmly boundaried scholarly time—as long as you are present and engaged at other times.

Be aware female and minority researchers! You may need to be especially alert to your own boundaries, in part because of the extra service foisted upon you. Whether it is to fulfill the role of the minority representative on a search committee or to function implicitly as the "go-to" person where specific human needs (e.g., consultation and empathy) are concerned, the reality is that one's gender and race can be a magnet for others' needs. Talk with other women and minority faculty to see how they handle an overabundance of requests from the institution: What life skills have they developed and what nuggets of wisdom can they impart that can help you?

Let's face it, new faculty can be expected to have their personal and professional boundaries tested, and in a variety of ways. The dynamics involved are not always troublesome but some faculty may feel pushed emotionally or intellectually, while others may be requested to do something suspicious or counter to policy; still others may be asked to share personal information about themselves in a way that feels invasive. Feeling exposed, awkward, or uncomfortable at different times and in different ways is probably common—but know yourself and what you can (or should) tolerate and what you should not. Early on, you'll need to get good at distinguishing between mere personality differences in the workplace and potential violations of human rights. Document uncomfortable situations, which range from harassment, to discrimination, to other forms of unethical conduct, such as sexism and racism; do not shy away from the party or parties involved. The idea is to try to prevent things from getting out of hand, so share your concerns. If the undesirable pattern should persist, pull in a third party with supervisory responsibility.

Professional conduct on your part does not mean putting blinders on and insulating yourself from the world. We would hope that the most productivity-minded among us would take action when and where needed. Only turtles get to live in a shell. However, being smart and knowing when to stand firm and over what issues is wholly different from seizing arms over every issue that pops up. Nurture both good boundaries and good judgment!

Know that others' boundaries are important, not just your own. Faculty mentors are not available 100 percent of the time, day and night, to attend to your needs, and neither is the university staff. While your faculty mentor, program coordinator, and department chair should all be invested in your success and well-being, they, too, must exercise boundaries if they are to get anything done at work. You will notice that everyone's tolerance for being interrupted is different; those in administrative and supervisory positions should have a higher threshold, largely because they have been hired to serve faculty and students. Actively discern and then clearly respect the mindset and work responsibilities of supervisors and colleagues.

Keep your professional exchanges with others short and focused, except where exploratory talk is preferable, and model how you'd like others to interact with you. It is respectful behavior to schedule meetings with faculty, administrators, and students and to expect the same courtesy in return; of course, some impromptu exchanges are unavoidable. We all spontaneously seek clarification to questions from our colleagues and turn to them to help with resolving unexpected issues. However, just as you will not want others to impose on you, do not be imposing yourself. It's often easy identifying obnoxious and intrusive behavior in colleagues and students. It is more difficult to detect and label the same behavior in ourselves.

16   Keep "To Do" Lists for Your Day, Year, and Career

Many highly productive academics keep "to do" lists for every day, month, and year. They also keep long-term plans in the form of lists or narratives of creative possibilities and potential projects. We find these varied types of lists to be indispensable in our own writing lives. Personal monitoring systems, including lists and calendars, help keep us organized, especially when we are feeling scattered with too many project demands. Such schedules and lists are essential for reminding ourselves what we need to accomplish in the busy days ahead.

Add your expanding lists to your day/month/year calendar or Palm Pilot. This way, critical writing and research activities, such as library trips, locating additional references for an article, conversations with specialists, and conference sessions will not be missed. And do not forget to keep track of long-term "dream" projects; these might include articles to write, book topics to explore, edited volumes to produce, publishing outlets to eventually target and anything else. One of us maintains a list of fully developed journal article titles for future exploration. The list includes anticipated coauthors and ideal dates for launching and completing each project. As the list grows and it becomes clear that not all of these projects are attainable, some are combined and others are dropped in favor of greater interest or higher priority manuscripts. One of us even keeps a folder for fiction ideas to be tackled during a future sabbatical!

Few academics keep a calendar reserved just for their writing and research. While some note "writing" in the blank spaces of their daily planners, this jotting is too vague, particularly for new faculty. Make visible to yourself (and maybe others) the time you have laid aside for writing and your commitment to research activity. We bet that if you were to study the calendars belonging to many of the academics around you, you'd find that writing is rarely scheduled. We've asked faculty we know if they schedule their writing in their date books. Most responded that they just try to remember to do it and that it's always at the back of their minds anyway. It's ironic that the most important activity in the academy, as far as tenure, promotion, and recognition in the field are concerned, is also the most invisible and haphazardly scheduled!

From our conversations with several prolific academics, we have distilled the following tips bearing on scheduling and tracking one's writing; we think each of these gems is worth passing along. First, prolific colleagues who are well organized keep a yearly planner for such major academic due dates as conference proposals, grant applications, and manuscript submission or revision. They want to be able to see the entire year at a glance. The importance of this practice for ensuring your sanity and productivity as an academician cannot be overstated. Without this careful macroview of your academic year, you cannot make wise decisions about which projects and how many of them you can reasonably take on. We know too many colleagues who say "yes" compulsively without thoughtfully considering their capacity to deliver within the contracted timeframe. Of course, they get swamped and worn down, and, upon failing to deliver, they stop getting invitations to write and receiving opportunities to publish.

Second, some single activities have numerous, time-sensitive commitments embedded within them, so design well-organized schedules that you can easily follow. Grant and conference activities are two such examples. Regarding conventions, you will need to carefully schedule all of those sessions you will be giving or attending, and all of those people you plan on meeting, in addition to the receptions and other events you wish to attend. We have found it essential to mark all such specifics in a custom-made schedule (hard copy or Palm Pilot), not just in the conference's thick program where one's sessions or meetings can be easily missed, especially when rushing.

Third, one's daily/monthly/yearly lists often serve as indispensable tools and helpful records for remembering and completing entries within one's annual reviews and promotional packages. Similarly, your annual list offers an opportunity to revisit your intended writing schedule and targeted writing projects after each year has expired. Did you accomplish your primary goals? Did manuscripts get submitted? Are you conspicuously behind on nearly everything you set out to write?

Use this information to reflect, re-evaluate, and troubleshoot. What factors inhibited your work? Why didn't the writing get done? Where did you allocate your time? Last, consider utilizing collaborative writing charts—especially when engaging in group projects with multiple authors or when writing with students. These charts show coauthors (faculty or students) the status of their project components and the progress being made (or not being made) on each. These charts should be frequently updated and circulated to all participants.

Accountability should be easier to uphold—and collegiality easier to maintain—when promises for collaborative work are displayed in the form of goals and specific target dates. This idea harkens back to Edwards Deming's notion of quality performance known as statistical process control (SPC). Deming's notion is summarized, "Your starting point towards a solution has to be a clear definition of the problems that the solution is supposed to improve" (Interested in SPC? Statistic Process Control, http://www.focus-spc.com/edwarddeming14point-theory, 2006.) In this case, the problem is that of organizing one's writing life and acting on one's commitment, and the solution is the display and tracking of promises. A graphic makes public the productivity that "workers" are making, whether collaboratively or separately. Such strategies can serve to motivate colleagues by clarifying where they are along the road to project completion and where they still need to go. Graphics can take the old-fashioned form of a plastic chart displayed in one's office where colored markers (or Post-it Notes) denote progress, or e-files can be alternatively used, replacing markers with colored fonts.

Although we have heretofore focused on long-term writing plans, we return now to the all-important task of planning your day. All prolific faculty desperately need to engage in explicit daily planning. With rare exceptions, the alternative to assiduous daily scheduling is poor productivity, scattered performance, and inconsistent follow-through with commitments. Like many other beginning professors, you may find your days, even weekends, disappearing into thin smoke as you tackle loads of e-mail messages, deal with unexpected teaching, advising, and administrative situations that arise, and attend to other—often low priority—work. Exhausted, because you are working hard at working hard, you may too infrequently get around to what matters—writing and the scholarly life. Don't put your writing on the backburner. Both of us have become profoundly mindful of our daily planners. We use these to block out a minimum of two full days of writing during the week—often a full day and two half days. We then try to block smaller chunks of time on the other days and we then use this schedule to protect our writing time from the guaranteed "creep" of external demands. We use our daily planners to get organized in advance for the various tasks to be accomplished. For example, when a writing block is scheduled, we make certain that other demands will not intrude and we come prepared with all the materials we need to get to work. And frankly, because professors are absentminded at times—especially when happily ensconced in a writing jag—we use our daytimers to remind ourselves about salient meetings, time with students, and more mundane errands.

The only person who can control your schedule is you. At the end of the day, only you and no one else but you can take credit for your productivity; the flip side is that you only have yourself to blame when well-laid (or poorly-laid) plans fall through. Carefully and thoroughly plan your writing, schedule your commitment to yourself, and act on it with high intention. None of us wants to be known as "listless."

3

CATER TO YOUR WRITING RHYTHMS

Take advantage of the days and times when you are most able to be productive. When your writing momentum is interrupted at work or at home, resume as soon as you can. Carefully observe your own biological "up" and "down" times and cater to these as a writer. When periods of "flow" occur, work to extend them as circumstances allow, and write in sync with your rhythms rather than against them. Finally, be cautious about substance-enhanced writing and monitor the broader health effects of substance use and sleep deprivation.

17   DISCOVER YOUR OPTIMAL WRITING TIME(S)

Of college professors, it is safe to say: No two are alike. As a fiercely independent and naturally idiosyncratic lot, academics truly march to the beat of their own drummers. Such individualism applies not only to the varied intellectual interests and emotional temperaments of professors, but also to their writing habits. Thus far we have encouraged you to write daily, to write on topics that fascinate you, to find your own best practices as a writer, to write in large blocks of time when possible, and to write "in the gaps" between blocks as well. But *when* should you write?

Honestly, it makes no more sense for us to tell you when you should engage in producing scholarship each day than it does for us to advise you when to eat, sleep, exercise, and teach. Nonetheless, there are some distinct variables to consider as you focus on the question of when; each merits attention and perhaps some personal experimentation before honing in on the ideal writing schedule. By far the most relevant variable to consider is your own biological clock. Each of us is driven to a large extent by a neurological and genetically linked sleep cycle. By now, you have probably identified yourself as an "early bird," a "night owl," or some creature in-between. Put simply, you wake up early and feel refreshed and alert in the morning or you stay up late and hit your stride later in the evening— perhaps doing your best work sometime after midnight. Of course, there are rare and enviable professors among us—often the youngest in the population of academics—who seem capable of both bird and owl behavior over long stretches without succumbing to outright exhaustion. But most of us are mortal and so we have no choice but to guard against writing at the expense of health.

Thus, part of writing effectively requires that you know your physical cycle. If an early bird, why not set you alarm for 5 A.M. every day and get about the business of writing several hours before any responsibilities kick in? If a night owl, why not plan to work until 2 A.M.—knowing you will sleep and teach later in the day? Erroneous information and old moralizing messages trip many of us up at first (e.g., staying up late is unhealthy, early risers are compulsive or depressed, night owls are lazy). Because there is no evidence to support any of these bits of common wisdom, we encourage you to discover your own time of maximal energy and clear focus for every day of the week, and to then schedule your writing during this period whenever possible. Over time, you may be able to schedule teaching, administrative duties, and even personal obligations around your optimal two- or three-hour daily writing slots.

Visualize a block of time as one stream, and optimal mental focus as another. By doing so, you should be able to see that, when brought together, the momentum of these two branches increases exponentially. Call this the *Confluence Model* of ideal writing time. Of course, depending upon your circumstances, you may need to take other tributaries into account. These may include other professional obligations, practical exigencies surrounding transportation, or even the need to work multiple jobs. Only you can determine, with any confidence, when you are likely to be at your peak writing performance each day. And only you can mold your schedule to accommodate this preference, your performance peak.

Another crucial variable in the conversation is your personal mix of family and possibly parental duties. Although you may be an early bird by nature, you may have an infant that finds early morning equally delightful and who chooses to greet each pre-dawn period with (or without) you. Or, you may find yourself, despite being a night owl, so exhausted most nights after rushing children or adolescents to various practices that you have little energy to start writing after their bed-time. Many of us also have ailing parents and in-laws living with us or at a distance who need our constant attention and care. Far from trivial, family obligations require important consideration when you try to tailor writing chunks to your own biological preference. Think of these as waterfalls and whirlpools in your writing stream. Thoughtfully anticipate them in order to save yourself angst later on.

18   WHEN IN THE "WRITER'S FLOW," STAY THERE!

If you are fortunate, you will sometimes find yourself in a nearly rapturous state of focus, clarity, and inspiration that lends itself thoroughly to breakthrough moments and quantum leaps in your progress on a piece of scholarship. Psychologists identify these mental states as "flow" periods, while professional athletes may describe it as being "in the zone." When you find yourself in the flow, the contour between work and pleasure dissolves; you can suddenly discern connections you have been seeking between disparate ideas, and a sense of producing words and ideas with ease makes the scholarly enterprise a delight. When the flow is particularly strong, you may find that your typing fingers can scarcely keep pace with your mental momentum. Whatever your moniker for these magical occasions, here is some advice: Don't end the session until you absolutely have to!

At times, the flow state can take on the flavor of nearly manic intensity. Although only about 1 percent of the population suffers from manic-depressive mood disorder, Pulitzer Prize-winning poets and other creative geniuses seem to be afflicted with the disorder at disproportionately high rates (Jamison, 1996). Vincent Van Gogh, Sara Teasdale, Virginia Wolfe, and Robert Louis Stevenson are good examples. In retrospect, such artists will often report doing their best and most productive work during the manic or highly energized phase of the illness. Although manic-depressive illness is a debilitating disorder, the notion of "going with the flow" when every day states of energy and creativity occur bears consideration. How often do academics prematurely terminate highly creative states and unique opportunities for genuine breakthroughs on projects merely because their writing timer goes off, signaling the end of a scheduled writing block?

Because most of us will not experience flow states daily or even weekly, it is important to stand ready to welcome and maintain them when they arrive. How can you keep yourself in the flow and, more important, keep the outside world at bay, while you ride the wave of productivity to its conclusion? Both of us experience being struck by flow states during the course of a distance run. Vague or previously hidden ideas germinate and take shape; mental vistas appear, allowing a sudden view of the entire landscape for an unwritten article or book. On those days, the author races back to the office, closes the door, and with exercise-induced endorphins fueling the process, enters the flow. In this state, an outline quickly takes shape; the writing occurs with ease, and hours tick by in a flash. We have colleagues who stimulate flow states by reading, gardening, or listening to music. Unfortunately, the magic spell is nearly always threatened by the exigencies of important obligations. Professional and personal demands rear their heads and the inevitable question arises: *Is there any way for me to gracefully excuse myself and stay with the flow?*

In our experience, far too few academic writers either recognize or honor flow states. To honor a red-hot writing state is to seek a graceful way to extricate yourself from immediate commitments so as to ride the muse as far as it will take you. Professors may believe they do not have permission to flex their schedules, or they may lack the assertiveness needed to excuse themselves from meetings or other scheduled events— even when outrageous productivity hangs in the balance. Remember: One of the true benefits of living the academic life is the profound freedom of discretionary time. Producing scholarship is a required part of the job description and annual assessment, so why place artificial constraints on when productivity can occur?

Having said this, we acknowledge that certain obligations of academe such as teaching, and the necessary preparation that accompanies good instruction and mentorship, cannot be compromised or shortchanged. But will it be catastrophic for you to on occasion miss a meeting, or reschedule a few appointments on an afternoon when the muse has set in something fierce and you are on the cusp of an extremely productive writing jag? Prolific writers quickly discern the distinction between flexibility in the service of productivity and irresponsibility. Here are two questions to ask when you find yourself in a quandary about staying in the flow or pulling back to attend to scheduled events. First, will anyone genuinely be adversely impacted by your occasional withdrawal from a meeting or rescheduling of an appointment? Second, will you be so distressed by doing so that the potential payoff in terms of writing will be negligible? Only you can answer these questions. If you find that zone or flow states are a frequent or predictable occurrence for you, you might consider informing colleagues and students that this is the case and ask for their kind indulgence in advance. Sometimes, informed consent can increase understanding and reduce resentment later on.

19   HONOR YOUR OWN WRITING RHYTHMS

Even though most productive academics tend to write every day and block chunks of time exclusively for writing each week, the fact remains that each will have a somewhat personal and idiosyncratic writing rhythm. One's writing rhythm is comprised of a signature set of biologic predispositions, psychological

preferences, and learned behavioral habits—each contributing
to the optimal circumstances and timing of productive writing.

One defining attribute of the writing rhythm is a preference
for writing in lengthy blocks versus narrower but perhaps more
frequent slices of time. We have already noted that writing "in
the gaps" as unanticipated opportunities present themselves
offers a strategic way to squeeze greater productivity from a
busy professorial schedule. But there are some among us who
always prefer shorter bursts of writing time to longer chunks.
Whether the result of a shorter span of focus, physical discomfort with longer periods of relative immobility, or a simple preference to "process" or "stew" frequently between jags of
writing, these authors will be more productive when they cater
to this rhythm. Of course, more academics seem to prefer
longer writing blocks. Both of your authors find it easiest to be
genuinely productive when we have time to wade into the
topic, get sufficiently immersed, and then plow through several
hours of writing with little interruption. Because this approach
caters to our strengths, we plan to stick with it!

Another stylistic component of writing rhythm has to do
with your preference or distaste for writing marathons—
especially when you are making marked progress on a project
and basking in the "flow," or when an editor or publisher's
deadline looms large. These required sessions are distinct from
the more modest blocks we discussed earlier. Whether you prefer slices or chunks of writing time, a marathon will involve sustained focus on a grant, article, or book chapter to the
exclusion of all else. Many academics—perhaps continuing a
time-honored practice from college and graduate school—pull
the traditional "all-nighter," or, as we age, the "late-nighter"
as a means of bulldozing through a project and achieving dramatic progress in a compressed time period. Of course, one's
physical and psychological stamina will place boundaries on
how effective such marathons will be and how frequently we
can engage in them.

And no discussion of writing marathons, stamina, and all-
nighters would be complete without some attention to the
problem of sleep and sleep deprivation among academics.
Increasingly, college professors are required to do more with

less. We are asked to teach more courses, mentor more students, and crank out more publications—all with the same mortal physical apparatus, the inflexible 24-hour day, and pressing demands in our personal lives. Although the ideal minimum sleep period each night for young to midlife adults is seven to nine hours, we know that many reading this guide may not remember the last time they got a full eight hours of sleep. As most of us have discovered at some point, a single night of poor sleep leads to fatigue or lethargy the following day. But an entirely sleepless night, several consecutive nights of minimal rest, or worse, a lifestyle of sleep deprivation, can lead to serious impairment in one's performance.

Indicators of severe sleep deprivation include extreme drowsiness, slowed physical and mental response times, irritability, depressed mood, poor physical coordination, a tendency to nod off during the day, and, after more extended periods of sleep deprivation, even hallucinations and delusional thoughts, as well as physical injury. The simple truth here is that borrowing from sleep time to increase productivity is likely to backfire when employed as a frequent strategy. Occasional marathons or all-nighters are probably not cause for concern. But a pattern of sleep loss will offer diminishing returns and may signal a problem with the writer's time management or unreasonable demands for superhuman productivity.

Variations in rhythms also pertain to macrofluctuations in your writing interest and intensity. That is, beyond your daily and weekly rhythms, you may find that you work very intensively for two weeks or until a project is completed. This may be followed by a phase of relative calm and comparatively little productivity (hopefully this phase will be quite brief!) as you consider your next project or simply catch your breath. Again, as long as you are not given to a lengthy hiatus following each piece of scholarship, there is little harm in catering to this preference for episodic downtime.

The environment or context for writing is another salient element of your ideal writing rhythm. Some professors learn early on that they are maximally productive when hidden away in a cloistered setting. Such locations may include a home office in the attic or basement, an anonymous cubical in the library, or a mountain cabin far from the nearest telephone. If you are quite prone to distraction or require this level of seclusion to write productively, then, by all means, cater to this preference and escape to your writing retreat routinely. There are many others among us who seem not only capable of writing effectively in a relatively busy environment, but actually seem to thrive on a constant backdrop of noise and activity. These professors write effectively sitting in a coffee shop, in a crowded city park, or even in their offices with the door propped open. Here is a certainty: Trying to write in an environment that fails to suit your contextual preferences will impede your work at best and halt it altogether at worst. On the other hand, don't wait to have things perfect all of the time, as your plans for productivity will only backfire. In other words, refrain from rationalizing that you could not get to the writing yesterday or today because of less-than-ideal writing circumstances. Our motto is: Adapt, adapt, adapt to the extent possible, and exert your will to tailor the setting as you would like where this is feasible.

And what about the little things like music, daylight, beverages, fresh flowers, laptops versus desktops, and comfortable clothing that can make all of the difference to writers? We classify these not-so-insignificant preferences as the *ergonomics of productive writing*. Ergonomics is the study of maximizing human performance through environmental design; attention to these preferences may nicely facilitate your work. Find the right chair (and back support) and desk for your writing; if you associate a good cup of coffee with writing, have a pot brewing before you get started, and if daylight or enticing vistas distract, then don't write in a location without blinds. One of us recently spent a year on sabbatical. Each writing day would begin early, clad in bathrobe, sipping coffee, and getting organized to make progress the minute the kids were off to the bus stop. The other has found that by duplicating the work-and-home environment with respect to Word software and computer programs, in addition to such apparatuses as back support cushions, a supply of decaffeinated coffee, and salient reference texts, a degree of seamlessness has occurred between these different writing spaces.

Find your own best writing rhythm and place to concentrate, uninterrupted. Cater to your need for sleep, honor the limits of your own stamina, search out the most conducive writing locations, arrange the environment to suit your tastes and preferences, create homework continuities that make writing seamless, and get to work.

20   STIMULATE BRAIN CHEMISTRY AND WRITING EFFICACY

We conclude this chapter on maintaining momentum and knowing yourself by offering a brief though candid look at brain chemistry and writing efficacy—what we call substance-accompanied writing. Whether the term *substance-facilitated* or *substance-impaired* writing is a better fit for you, we encourage you to carefully consider this issue.

No treatment of writing and chemistry could begin anywhere other than with Starbucks, or perhaps with any coffee purveyor. To be fair, college students and professors the world over use not only coffee, but also tea, caffeinated soda, anti-drowsiness pills, energy drinks, nuts, and even heavy-duty doses of chocolate to achieve some level of caffeine stimulation. Not only is caffeine a ritualized and revered facet of academic culture, many academics find themselves using increasing doses of the drug in order to stave off sleep, maintain focus, extend writing marathons, and stimulate creative thinking. One of us must disclose having an office coffee maker that is rarely turned to the *off* position during a workday. This author has learned from hard experience that caffeine intake must be cut-off in the early evening if sleep is to occur normally, and that too much caffeine can quickly lead to unpleasant physical symptoms. The other author quit caffeine intake altogether several years ago at the doctor's request, which almost immediately resulted in improved health.

In moderation, coffee and associated beverages can offer a positive chemical boost for meeting the writing challenge. It holds the added benefit of serving as a delightful occasion-and-format for interaction with students and faculty colleagues. But like all magical elixirs, caffeine has a downside that many of us deny until problems set in. The American Psychiatric Association's manual of diagnoses notes that *caffeine intoxication*—often induced by sustained and heavy use of the drug—can quickly instigate such symptoms as restlessness, nervousness, insomnia, frequent urination, gastrointestinal disturbance, muscle twitching, rambling flow of thought and speech, heart palpitations, sweating, cardiac arrhythmia, and psychomotor agitation. Certainly, sleep deprivation and heart arrhythmias can become cause for medical attention. The message is simple, be attuned to your own response to stimulants and pay attention to increasing use and the symptoms just noted.

The other substance worth mentioning briefly here is alcohol. When not hoisting a cup of tea or a triple espresso, how many professors—typically when working at home—pour themselves a glass of wine, a beer, or something stiffer? In our experience, this practice is not altogether atypical. Alcohol may serve many functions for the writer. It may induce relaxation and thereby disinhibit the author; it may quell serious anxiety about achieving tenure or promotion, or about one's capacity to get published at all, and alcohol may simply create a desirable and disinhibited state from which to create. Whatever the motivation for "mixing" drinking with writing, we simply recommend caution. Most adults, including college professors, who are eventually diagnosed with alcohol dependence describe a slowly evolving decline into the illness. Famous horror author Stephen King (2000) has done us all a favor by deftly recording his own struggle with alcoholism while at the peak of his writing career:

> In the eighties, Maine's legislature enacted a returnable bottle and can law. Instead of going into the trash, my sixteen-ounce cans of Miller Lite started going into a plastic container in the garage. One Thursday night I went out there to toss in a few dead soldiers and saw that this container, which had been empty on Monday night, was now almost full. And . . . I was the only one in the house who drank Miller Lite. My nights during the last five years of my drinking always ended with the same ritual.

I'd pour any beers left in the refrigerator down the sink. If I didn't, they'd talk to me as I lay in bed until I got up and had another. And another. And one more. (pp. 94–95, 96)

Unlike drinking and driving, drinking and writing is permissible (except on dry college campuses). But if you *must* drink to write or decompress, or should alcohol intake increase, look in the mirror and ask why. Keep in mind that alcohol is a powerful central nervous system depressant. While initially disinhibiting, it will eventually lead to drowsiness, fatigue, and slowed cognition—brain cells die. And for goodness sake, we academics need all the brain cells we can summon forth! On a more serious note, remind yourself on occasion that chronic alcohol abuse is correlated with liver disease and a particularly heart-rending form of dementia—Korsokoff's Syndrome. We can imagine nothing worse for the typical academic than the irreversible memory decline characteristic of this alcoholism-induced disorder.

Respect the slippery slope of substance-accompanied writing. Exercise control—only a fine line exists between talking to the bottle and responding when "it" talks to you.

4

DEVELOP THE ATTITUDES
AND PERSPECTIVES OF
A PROLIFIC WRITER

Know what mental frames or mindsets you bring to the expectation to produce publishable scholarship. Do you see writing as a burden, or as a privilege? In this chapter, we encourage you to adopt the attitude that writing is a privilege. You may need to overcome fears associated with writing by digging deep to find alternatives to such feelings that are rooted in a genuine love of scholarship. Patience, for instance, is a fundamental virtue for the successful scholar and you must foster it if you are to learn to cope with the many tasks, demands, and experiences of academic work. Another important characteristic of the productive writer is persistence, which is much needed in the face of rejection from editors and publishers; one also perseveres when obstacles, unpleasant outcomes, and resistance are encountered and dealt with. Unless you can tolerate rejection and learn from the process, you will have a very difficult time. The more tolerant of rejection you are, the less defensive you will feel about reviewer and editorial feedback and the less procrastinating you will do as a writer. Also, prolific writers learn effective coping skills not only with respect to peer-reviewed rejections but also to the demands on their time and setbacks in writing; develop your capacity to effectively manage stress and deal with obstacles. Finally, prolific writers take time to contemplate the bigger picture and the abiding meaning in their writing.

21   Frame Productivity as
a Professional Privilege

If there is a single area of your inner attitudinal world that is destined to determine whether you join the ranks of genuinely prolific scholars or wallow in a perpetual state of scholarly underachievement, it is the lens or perspective you use to frame your writing and the mindset you bring to it. In our experience, there are two rather clear options for conceptualizing your scholarly writing—think of these as cognitive schemas or perceptual grids through which your thoughts about writing must pass. Of course, your choice of schema will dramatically impact the emotions and behaviors that accompany the various components of productive writing.

The first option is to view academic writing as an odious demand and burdensome duty—call this the reluctant writer, resistant scholar, or resentful professor camp. Sadly, if this schema persists, the moniker "perpetual assistant professor" might also fit. No matter where you are employed, we think this view of the universal and time-honored requirement to produce scholarship in order to achieve promotion is a disservice to both yourself and your institution. Research in cognitive psychology indicates that when any activity or relationship is framed as an onerous obligation, enjoyment of the activity declines, resentment bubbles up, and an angry or sullen demeanor becomes evident when the person is confronted with the demands of the activity or relationship. Not surprisingly, behavioral resistance also ensues; whether conscious or unconscious, the person will begin to avoid, make excuses, procrastinate, or even rail against the perceived duty. When a love relationship moves from treasured privilege to unfair burden in the mind of the lover, few are surprised when the relationship dissolves. When the reality of scholarly expectations in academe feels like an unreasonable or dreaded demand, we are not surprised that some college professors become ambivalent, resentful, and unsuccessful in the academy.

In contrast to this grudging attitudinal or cognitive framework is the second camp—call this the consummate professor, the appreciative academic, or the responsible colleague; in time, he or she will also be called full professor. The prolific professor frames the expectation for scholarship as a privilege that accompanies the status of college professor. One of the most respected professions in most societies, college professors have long enjoyed a unique measure of vocational status, societal respect, discretionary time, and genuine freedom when teaching and writing. Recent U.S. polls indicate that college professor is the second-most desirable and fulfilling profession known to Americans. In return, professors are expected to be learned, invested in their students, unequivocally fair, and active contributors to the reservoir of knowledge through original research and writing; they must be productive scholars in whatever way productivity is defined in their unique disciplines. When academics view themselves as fortunate participants in this time-honored and, quite frankly, privileged society of scholars, they are more likely to see sacred tradition and rich opportunity in the call to create in and contribute to their field.

There are also some practical reasons for framing productivity as a professional privilege. First, most definitions of competence—at least as they apply to college professors—incorporate the notions of active engagement with the discipline, maintaining cutting-edge expertise in one's specialties, and contributing to the fund of knowledge through original scholarship. Second, vibrant and effective role models and mentors to students are tied-in and actively engaged scholarly contributors. It is difficult to lead others where you yourself have never traveled; credible teaching and mentoring demand first hand and recent experience as a scholar. It is a privilege to be able to contribute to the field with which you identify and an honor to own the mantel of expert and guide for future generations. A third pragmatic reason for framing your scholarly work as a privilege is the simple fact that productive scholars enjoy numerous advantages and opportunities in their careers, including positive attention from colleagues and employers, invitations to travel and speak, grant funding to do more of what one already enjoys, peer-bestowed awards from prestigious associations, and a sense of gratification associated with making a noteworthy mark in one's field.

When a professional athlete or an elected official takes the field or assumes office, there is a reasonable expectation among fans and constituents that the professional or public servant will give it everything he or she's got. In exchange for the privilege of occupying an esteemed—and often quite competitive—occupational station, in response to being entrusted with the institution's reputation, and in light of the sacred trust students offer to revered professors, fulfilling the expectation of scholarly activity can easily be framed as a professional privilege. If you are an academician, we believe you owe it to your students, your colleagues, your dean and college president, your academic discipline, and most important yourself, to embody the values espoused here and to be highly productive.

22 WRITE TO THRIVE, NOT MERELY TO SURVIVE

Once you have adopted the attitude that writing is a privilege rather than an onerous demand, it is time to do away with any vestige of another pernicious and self-defeating mindset common among new academic writers—writing simply to avoid perishing. One of the early titles for this book was *Publish or Perish!* We initially thought the title might appeal to the universal concerns among academics about achieving tenure and establishing a track record as a scholar certain to lead to promotion. After some careful reflection, we decided the title was entirely off base; it catered to a writing mentality rooted in fear. In our estimation, far too many new professors are doing what we refer to as *writing scared*; they turn to scholarly pursuits as a means of avoiding failure and clinging to their jobs.

When a professor writes scared, he or she can scarcely be distinguished—at least in psychological terms—from any other laborer in an environment of job cuts and a declining economy. Here the employee works like mad to salvage his or her job, outperform the nearest competitors, and convince skeptical managers to keep him or her on the payroll for another month. This worker knows pervasive anxiety, feels continuously threatened, and operates from a basic and uncomfortable position of defensive self-protection.

For anyone reading this guide who finds this description of occupational life all too familiar in the academy, we encourage one of two options: (1) make a profound and deliberate shift in your attitude about writing, or (2) look for another, more suitable career. If you are writing scared—working hard at cranking out publications merely to avoid the tenure or promotion axe—we challenge you to ask yourself: Is this really worth it? Is this what I bargained for? Am I happy? We suspect the answer to these questions may be "no." Here is a paradox about fear-induced writing: Although fear can sometimes be a powerful motivator—sometimes even propelling a scholar to achieve tenure—fear simultaneously undermines joy. In the lexicon of human emotions, joy and anxiety are incompatible. They cannot coexist (except in Schizophrenia or other altered states). If your primary emotional frame for the scholarly enterprise is anxiety, then do not be surprised when you fail to anticipate or find delight in many of the tasks associated with writing. Fear undermines enjoyment. When publishing to avoid perishing, expect work to be work.

The alternative to fear-induced writing is writing rooted in a genuine love of scholarship, a cognitive framework that casts expectations for productivity as welcome challenges, and a take on producing work that goes something like this: "I write prolifically because it's part of who I am; research, writing, teaching, and service to my profession are all intertwined at the level of my very identity as a professor." Call this *writing to thrive*. In this case, writing is not a desperate act designed to aid in survival, but an activity that caters to intellectual curiosity, needs for achievement, and joy at accomplishing creative feats. This cognitive shift may be avoided by taking time to reflect existentially about why you pursued an academic career in the first place.

Of course, there are times when thriving academics do not enjoy writing. And there are times when they worry about getting tenured and days when they see more work than play in sitting down and writing. Both of your authors have had these moments, days, and even weeks. Both of us worried about getting to the next promotional plateau and felt compelled to crank out a few "insurance" pubs as the date for tenure review drew close. But here is a telling sign about our more consistent motivation for writing: After we were tenured and promoted, we continued writing—a lot—and more ambitious and high-risk products have resulted! Rather than frame tenure as a ticket to check out as scholars, we framed tenure as an opportunity to write for the joy of writing, and as an opportunity to write about whatever pleased us. Prolific scholars write like crazy even when they achieve some job security and fear-based incentives fade away. Successful scholars would often feel lost or at least aggravated, perhaps unfulfilled, if prevented from engaging in the craft for long—even in non-tenure track positions.

To enjoy your *entire* career as an academician—especially those first five or six pre-tenure years—recognize and confront your own fear-induced writing behavior. Frame writing as an opportunity to achieve, create, establish a scholarly niche, and draw positive attention to yourself and your institution.

23   BE PATIENT AS A SCHOLARLY WRITER

Patience is a fundamental virtue for successful scholars. Because many of the tasks, demands, and experiences of the academic writer are tedious, frustrating, or disappointing, unshakable patience is crucial. When writing becomes painfully monotonous, when students or collaborators are late with their contributions, and when terse or mean-spirited editors not only reject your work but also suggest that it may indeed be the worst they've ever seen, you must have some staying power, some equanimity, and some forbearance. Think of patience as both a personality attribute and a character virtue that is evident in certain behaviors of the writer. We believe scholarly writers can nurture and deliberately practice patience.

There are several aspects of patience that committed writers should consider. Patience is manifest in a calm, steadfast demeanor and in the capacity to effectively regulate and appropriately express emotional states. One of the key features of *emotional intelligence* (Goleman, 1995) is self-regulation—the ability to both understand one's own emotions and then modulate or regulate appropriate expression of that emotion. An emotionally unregulated writer is prone to impulsive states or expressions of anger and fits of irritability. We have both seen colleagues with poor self-regulation become enraged at editors or coauthors when manuscripts have been rejected or extremely punitive and shaming toward students or collaborators when deadlines were missed. Of course, the net effect of this behavior is the writer's own ostracism. Editors will remember angry, sarcastic, or patronizing retorts from authors, sharply diminishing authors' chances of getting something accepted next time. (This is not a knock on editors, merely recognition that we are all human.) And what colleague or graduate student, editor or publisher wants anything to do with an impatient, especially demanding, collaborator or advisor? A tantrum is a tantrum—whether thrown by a two-year-old or a middle-aged professor. In sum, the emotionally unregulated academic sabotages his or her own long-term success and significantly reduces the probability of publication success.

Beyond the virtue of emotional calm, a key aspect of patience is the capacity to endure hardship and adversity, to keep moving ahead in difficult circumstances without quitting or engaging in inordinate griping. We can't begin to describe the number of things in our own writing lives that demand this kind of patient forbearance. Good examples of major events that impacted our writing and required our patience, within the last year alone, include:

1. Colleagues who fail to get their part of a joint article to us on time
2. Contributors to edited volumes who eagerly promise a chapter by a specific deadline and then disappear, fail to deliver, and become harder to contact than someone in a witness protection program
3. Acts of mother nature (e.g., hurricanes and snow storms), as well as computer breakdowns, and power outages
4. Indecisive journal editors who required four reviews and revisions of a short article resulting in a 2.5 year delay in publication
5. A journal editor who, after a long period of review, outright rejected a thoroughly revised article that had been provisionally accepted

6. Days—and more than a few late nights—when not a single coherent thought or sentence seems to come, nor the motivation to dig deep enough to find something of value
7. Sick children, the death of one of our parents, a grandmother, and an aunt, personal illnesses that affected overall health in addition to writing concentration and productivity, and the sudden requirement for lengthy, post-injury physical therapy appointments several times weekly
8. Repeated rejections of a book proposal
9. Departmental issues and subsequent reorganization that had a significant toll personally and professionally

Your own list of frustrating events, obstacles to writing, problematic colleagues, and annoying student behavior will undoubtedly be just as long as ours. In fact, it is reasonable to suggest that obstacles and disappointments, often of a changing nature, are a guaranteed "nuisance," if not permanent facet of the writing life.

A final element of patience is a stalwart refusal to make unreasonable demands—of self, others, and the larger world. Many of the things that frustrate us as writers are directly linked to human imperfection—both our own and that of almost everyone we work with! It is true that to err is human. It is also human to get bogged down in too many projects and commitments, to get behind, to be too critical or not empathic enough when giving authors feedback, to get bored, and to fail at some of the things we try. Reasonably fulfilled scholars eschew perfectionist demands for flawless performance while striving for excellence. It is easier to be patient when your internal dialogue goes something like, "I'd really prefer that all my contributors are on time with their manuscripts, but it's not catastrophic if a few are behind. Yes, I may have to birddog some writers, drop others altogether, and do some last minute writing of my own, but in the end, my work and this volume will go on." In our experience, this has worked much better than alternatives such as, "Damn it, everyone better be on time or else this whole thing is ruined and those responsible should suffer in hell. Because of the irresponsibility of others, I'll end up having to scrap the whole thing."

The question seems straightforward enough but only time will tell: How patient and self-regulated will you be in response to the guaranteed hassles as well as unavoidable obstacles to your best-laid writing plans?

24 Be Persistent as a Scholarly Writer

Although prolific scholars tend to be extraordinary intellects, many are most distinguished by their willingness to be systematic and persistent. This is particularly true when a manuscript or book proposal is rejected—a frequent experience for most junior academics. Defined as a refusal to quit or give up when the work gets monotonous or feels overwhelming, persistence is among the most important characteristics of any successful academic and productive writer. Persistence requires a measure of emotional and psychological endurance; the persistent scholar keeps on writing in spite of obstacles, unpleasant outcomes, and internal or external resistance.

Doggedness, perseverance, and tenacity are characteristic of nearly all great writers—including those in the world of fiction. It may be heartening to know that John Grisham had his first novel rejected by 16 agents and a dozen publishing houses before an agent finally gave him the green light. His first novel sold only 5,000 copies—hardly a great literary success. How easy it might have been to quit. But Grisham persisted. And then there is the acclaimed horror novelist Stephen King. As an adolescent, writing and submitting story after story, he began sticking each new rejection slip onto a large nail he hammered to his bedroom wall: "By the time I was fourteen (and shaving twice a week whether I needed to or not) the nail in my wall would no longer support the weight of the rejection slips impaled upon it. I replaced the nail with a spike and went on writing" (King, 2000, p. 41). You get the idea: folks who make it big as writers share the behavioral characteristic of dogged persistence. Now, persistence in the absence of talent may not get an academic far, but we believe that persistence, combined with even modest ability and knowledge of one's research paradigm or field, is strongly correlated with prolific scholarship.

In the life of a prolific academic, persistence takes many forms. These writers are persistent about scheduled writing time, for example. They continue to write when they experience job hassles, personal setbacks, or when they feel especially bored or disenchanted with a project to which they have committed themselves. They keep up the momentum when colleagues leave them hanging with unfinished tasks, when publishers shoot down their best ideas, and when a much anticipated data set refuses to yield any significant results.

But more than anything else, prolific writers are persistent in the face of rejection. These academics take negative editorial decisions in stride, or perhaps, more honestly, keep their reactions to rejections in check, refusing to feel wounded, personally diminished, or enraged. To the contrary, they carefully consider the feedback, modify the manuscript as indicated or recommended by the editor and reviewers, and immediately submit it to the second-choice outlet. They follow this same process if the manuscript is rejected a second or third time, on each occasion gleaning new insight that improves their work. Academics with lengthy lists of publications have learned—hopefully early on—that absolute determination in the face of uncertainty with respect to manuscript review pays off with eventual publication.

One of the reasons that persistence is so central to increasing the probability of publication is that editors are human; we must remember they've faced some of the same academic and professional challenges as the rest of us. These people have walked in your shoes themselves before gaining tenure and ascending to the editorship of a journal in their field. When a cordial, collegial author responds to an editor's "revise and resubmit" letter with a thoroughly modified manuscript and a cover letter that expresses appreciation for the guidance received, one that carefully outlines each modification in the revision, an editor cannot help but be impressed. And when the author responds to more than one round of revisions with the same equanimity and attitude of cooperation, it may be hard for an editor not to be won over; slowly, he or she may become an advocate of the author's work, transitioning from gatekeeper to helper to writing coach. Editors and publishers are not typically viewed as writing coaches even though the best of them are or can be. But when they have the opportunity to work with persistent and responsive authors, it may be difficult to resist the temptation to offer assistance of a constructive nature.

25 TOLERATE REJECTION
(AND LEARN FROM IT)

Unless you can tolerate rejection and learn from the process, your tenure in academe will be short (and miserable). Many of the refereed journals to which you will submit your work accept only a small fraction of manuscripts. Even elite scholars experience rejection, having to significantly revise their writing in addition to sequentially submitting their work to several journals before receiving a favorable response. What does it mean to *tolerate* rejection? To tolerate anything is to:

1. Allow without prohibiting or opposing
2. To recognize and respect
3. To endure
4. To put up with something or somebody unpleasant

In order to thrive as a writer, you must become a master in the art of toleration, turning rejection into something positive.

If you are extremely sensitive to rejection, undone by criticism, or depressive instead of disappointed when things do not go your way, you will need to actively change your perspective or exit academe altogether. We hope that you choose the former. If you struggle with anticipatory fear about or difficulty responding effectively following rejection, here are some things to consider. First, is your maladaptive reaction to rejection a pervasive problem? Unfortunately, some new academics hail from backgrounds that sensitized them to feel shamed and diminished by any perceived failure. Quite often, rejection intolerance is part of a pervasive pattern of perfectionism. The academic makes unreasonable demands for flawless performance in most areas of life—especially those domains with an evaluative component. Perfectionism and demands that one never fail may work for a talented graduate student, but even the brightest professor—assuming that he or she is at times submitting scholarship for review to the top journals—will at least occasionally have work rejected. This is the nature of the publishing "beast," so to speak.

A second problem with fear of rejection is that it often creates fertile soil for procrastination. The procrastinating scholar is immobilized, circling in a perpetual holding pattern and apparently unable to sit down and get the writing done. In reality, the procrastinator is often fearful of failure; he or she is unwilling to risk further rejection. At the root of procrastinating are potent irrational beliefs such as: "I can't stand any more rejection," or "It is awful when a colleague points out problems with my work." Of course, on logical, scientific, and pragmatic grounds, these beliefs are ridiculous (e.g., where is the evidence that you can't tolerate a little rejection and how does it follow that because it's not pleasant to hear about the weaknesses in your work that hearing about them ranks as "awful"?). Quite often, fear of rejection is an unconscious motivator for procrastinating. We hope that bringing it to the surface here will make this motivation conscious and therefore a less potent force in the lives of those for whom it is an issue.

Poor rejection tolerance can also signal a tendency to erroneously personalize reviewer and editorial feedback. Upon receiving a negative decision or particularly caustic and terse reviewer comments, it is easy for academics to imagine that the reviewer or editor holds particular disdain or specifically malignant intent toward the author. Of course, this thinking is humorously grandiose and rarely true. In our experience, editors and reviewers are very busy and scarcely have time to do their jobs without taking extra time to deviously craft feedback letters designed to deflate or disturb authors. Although some reviewers and editors could be more thoughtful and encouraging in their feedback, most have an innate and palpable interest in coaching and offering consultation in the course of their work. Here is the bottom line: Don't let your ego or worth as a writer hinge on receiving accolades and acceptances every time you submit your work. Be your own best supporter and be realistic.

When it comes to handling rejection, it may be useful to equate rejection of your scholarly work with rejection in romantic relationships. Some junior scholars respond like dysfunctional jilted lovers to manuscript rejection; some become withdrawn and asocial, some become bitter and suspicious—expecting and reacting strongly to rejection each time it occurs, and a few may become stalkers—endlessly haranguing or arguing with editors so that they effectively sabotage any chance of future success.

So, how can you respond adaptively to the scholarly rejections you will almost certainly rack up during your career? First, inoculate yourself to rejection by reading this section several times after submitting your work and before receiving a response from the editor. Second, when the decision letter arrives and if the decision is negative, or should major revision be required, tuck the reviews in the file folder containing this manuscript and put the folder away for a few days. We find that this "time out" strategy is great for preventing such irrational reactions as anger or self-deprecating. After a few days (or sooner, as you become more resilient and adaptive to rejection), look at the file: Slowly read the editor's letter and every word in the accompanying reviews. Then read everything again, this time underlining or highlighting salient requirements and recommendations. Know your work and gnaw at it: In the words of American author David Henry Thoreau, "Pursue, keep up with, critical round and round your life. Know your own bone: gnaw at it, bury it, unearth it, and gnaw at it still" (cited in Dillard, 1989, p. 68). Third, frame these documents as free and valuable feedback (constructive response truly is a gift) designed to improve your work and enhance your chances of publication. Recognize that you are getting an opportunity to improve as a writer while collecting crucial intelligence about the journal and the preferences or "personality" of the specific editor. If this is an important journal in your field, this information will be crucial to your long-term success. Fourth, mindfully reflect over time on the rejections you receive on your various manuscripts and work to discern any patterns among the rejections, or common causes for them. Is there something about your writing style you need to correct? Do you tend to submit work with sloppy errors or grammatical deficits? Are there serious methodological problems with your research or insufficient theoretical grounding for your ideas? Are generalizations or claims being made without sufficient support and evidence? When more than one journal editor says the same thing in the course of rejecting your work, it behooves you to take note and translate this counsel into significant changes in your approach. Empower yourself to reflect, learn, and change how you approach academic writing: Take off the blinders and gnaw on your bone.

We all may know stories of academics and especially great writers who have experienced rejection to the point of crisis at some point in their lives. From the literary world, take Thoreau for example, famous for the classic *Walden*, which explores natural simplicity, harmony, and beauty as conditions for social existence. Years earlier while at Walden Pond he had written *A Week on the Concord and Merrimack Rivers*, an elegy to his brother. When a publisher for the work could not be secured, Thoreau published it himself, a poor decision that devastated him financially. But after that, while paying off his debts, he continuously revised his other manuscript. In 1854 *Walden* (also known as *Life in the Woods*) was published, recounting his two-year venture at Walden Pond (*Wikipedia*, 2006).

As a caveat, we acknowledge that top journals and editors have certainly been known to initially reject groundbreaking and innovative work deserving of public attention. Sometimes, scholars that change the course of a discipline are outcasts in their first efforts to publish pioneering perspectives on a discipline or field. But if you are a relatively new academic, we encourage you to learn to tolerate rejection, refrain from envisioning yourself as a scholarly, award-winning genius, and, where it makes good sense, humbly heed the advice of reviewers and editors. Remember, academics who are adept at writing and reviewing are usually able to figure out how novice and even expert writers can improve their work and in ways not readily discernible to the writer him- or herself, at least not for some time.

26 Learn Good Coping Skills as a Writer

Prolific writers learn early on to cope effectively with numerous demands on their time, setbacks in writing progress, and rejections from editors and funding sources. Although we encourage prevention whenever possible, it is rarely possible to prevent many of the stressors that impinge on the typical academic's experience. Therefore, your capacity to effectively manage stress and move beyond obstacles will help to predict how effective you will be at getting material written and published.

In order to effectively manage academic stressors, you will need to make accurate appraisals of the stressful events themselves. Two crucial phases exist in the process of accurate appraisal (Lazarus & Folkman, 1984). In the primary appraisal phase, adaptive writers must decide whether an event is a direct threat (likely to cause harm or damage) or merely a challenge (although difficult or unpleasant, the event may yield some gain). Because we have rarely heard of homicidal students, administrators, or editors, and because most authors are confronted with stressors in the relative safety of their own offices, we think it reasonable to assume that most of your stressors will appropriately be framed as challenges. Ironically, however, many otherwise reasonable academics react to rejection letters and other challenges as though they were direct threats to life and limb—their sympathetic nervous system kicks in, blood pressure spikes, and, on a physiological level, they are preparing to fight or run for their lives.

Stressful events in the writer's life are not always external, of course, as in the case of the anxiety or at least restlessness many of us feel when trying to rouse that "peculiar internal state which ordinary life does not induce" (p. 46). Contemporary novelist Annie Dillard (1989) humorously goes on to say that writers do not have it easy—we must find within ourselves the fortitude and strength to prepare ourselves for this state all on our own, without having recourse to the communal rituals of a Zulu warrior or Aztec maiden. A work in progress that is neglected becomes harder to manage and control, Dillard adds, because the work—a wild, uncaged "lion"—will take control over our lives, forcing us to tiptoe around it unless we assert our mastery. We learn good coping skills as a writer by writing every day and by taking control of this activity, not letting it dominate us.

After you have correctly identified writing obstacles and setbacks as challenges, the second phase of accurate appraisal, secondary appraisal, involves estimating your capacity to respond effectively to the situation. In the secondary phase of coping, you will be asking yourself such questions as: Do I have the ability to remedy the problem? Will any effort or strategy on my part make a difference? Do I have the resources or contacts to get past this problem? In general, when a scholar encounters a problem or stressor, correctly interprets it as a challenge rather than an insurmountable threat, and then moves to appraise what will be required to effectively respond, the author is engaging in *problem-focused coping*. Problem-focused copers act calmly, directly, and proactively to tackle the situation and improve it. They see the problem as a challenge, believe they have the capacity to address it effectively, appraise the situation thoroughly but only to the extent necessary, and quickly take steps to do so.

Strategies of problem-focused coping in the wake, say, of having a major scholarly product rejected by a journal, include these actions:

1. Putting the material away briefly to gather one's thoughts, recognizing that a single rejection does not define either the author or the work
2. Gathering information about issues raised in the feedback and carefully considering an effective response
3. Consulting with experienced colleagues regarding both the work itself and well-matched outlets
4. Building networks of peers willing to offer social support, encouragement, and thorough copyediting or proofreading
5. Ensuring the prevention of maladaptive responses by engaging in good self-care, arranging ongoing social support, and thinking in advance about adaptive responses to possible rejections

The alternative to problem-focused coping, *emotion-focused* coping, occurs when we identify a stressful situation or setback as impossible, unmanageable, or beyond repair. We have both seen emotion-focused coping among colleagues—typically in response to failed early attempts at publication or grant support. Emotion-focused coping among academics results in giving up and developing a syndrome called *learned-helplessness*, in which a writer begins to believe that nothing he or she does will result in success; this individual faults others as saboteurs, assumes future failure, capitulates, and ceases the problem-focused coping behaviors that will likely result in a reversal of one's fortunes. A vast proportion of prolific scholars cope with initial failures by editing, rewriting, and seeking consultation, and repeating this cycle of refinement until they discover highly effective strategies for getting their work successfully and safely through the publishing gauntlet.

27   Take Time (But Not Your Writing Time) to Contemplate

Productive scholarship is both a privilege and an expectation for those of us occupying academic jobs. Prolific scholars are patient, persistent, and adaptive in their response to setbacks; they write to thrive, not merely to keep their jobs or to look good to an external party. But there is one more dimension of the attitude and element in the practice of prolific writers that bears discussion here. Prolific writers take time to think about their work—not just mechanical details, drafts, or data analysis, but the bigger picture and the abiding meaning in their writing. Call this the contemplative aspect of the healthy academic's psychology.

Conscientious contemplation in the life of a writer serves at least two essential purposes. First, periods of contemplation allow some internal reflection about one's line of scholarship, where it seems to be headed, and whether the author maintains genuine interest and purpose in the work at hand. Salient questions for self-reflection include: Does this area still exert a gravitational pull on me? Do I find meaning in all the hard work largely because the potential contribution is significant? Do I find joy in studying this topic and writing about it? Is this subject so infused with intrigue and meaning that I can imagine sticking with it for the long-term? Is my interest in this area of scholarship still something that gets me up in the morning and preoccupies me to the point of absorption? Has my line of inquiry reached a proverbial dead end such that continuing to push ahead would be fruitless? At some point along the journey did the balance shift so that writing is mostly work with very little joy—in a word, drudgery? Is now the right time to consider making a major shift in specific focus or methodology, or is it time to move to an entirely different area of scholarship altogether? Am I reasonably productive yet somehow disconnected from the work?

Obviously, these are weighty questions that go directly to the heart of a writer's existential well-being. Each has bearing on the emotional, spiritual, and philosophical peace and meaning you are likely to experience during the writing enterprise. And it should also be apparent that these questions are easily ignored by busy academics or academics in denial about waning interest in their own work. The contemplative academic must ask and reflect on these questions, or questions like them, episodically, and to be efficacious, they must be answered honestly. It might be that many prolific scholars who find their work meaningful and motivating are also transparent with themselves and proactive about making changes in response to internal and external triggers. We know of major figures in our own educational disciplines who excel at both recognizing and incorporating emergent trends into their lines of inquiry without steadfastly holding on to outdated concepts and research topics.

The second purpose behind contemplation involves brainstorming, imagining, and visualizing the contours of your next manuscript, your next line of research, or even an entirely new scholarly focus. In the day-to-day rush to teach, attend meetings, interact with students, and squeeze in writing blocks, it is easy to overlook these crucial opportunities for creative contemplation. We think of these as revitalizing moments and have found it important to have pen and paper ready so that when fledgling ideas are birthed, we can put them to paper immediately and nurture them through continued reflection and creative visioning.

For anyone so predisposed, keeping a journal of creative contemplation about ideas or directions for future scholarship is a good idea. Journaling allows the academic to sketch out ideas and plans that are in progress and watch them develop naturally, and without the intimidation of a blank computer screen. This writing process provides a workspace for describing ideas and concepts, philosophizing beyond situations, expressing feelings, and problem solving. Write freely or use categories that are meaningful to you for eliciting and organizing your thoughts. Moreover, consider analyzing your journal for themes as you develop material. In addition to this, we also write overviews of what we have learned and incorporate all that works into our academic writing. Any and all of these processes can be undertaken alone or with a collaborator. Every encounter with one's self or one's psyche, whether through journaling or brainstorming, should become an experience in stimulation, invigoration, and contemplation. Any creative conception needs the writer to look beyond, simultaneously drawing cues from outside one's self and from within.

We, Brad and Carol, have routinely engaged in both summative and formative forms of contemplation over the course of our careers—although like many of our busy colleagues, we sometimes neglect these opportunities for too long. Important contemplative moments have occurred for us early in the morning when sipping tea or coffee and thinking about the days, weeks, and months ahead, on the drive to work, when jogging during the day, or when chatting with our favorite students during research meetings. Some academics will do well to schedule periodic time for reflection and scholarship planning, and others operate more effectively by seizing opportune moments whenever they arrive.

Both of us have honed a contemplative ritual that has served us well over the years. Whenever an important article, book chapter, or book is published and finally arrives in our mailbox at work, we try to take an hour or two—ideally that day—to walk to a waterfront coffee shop in town or a nearby Starbucks on campus, and read (or skim as the case may be) the work in detail. Not only is this ritual deeply satisfying— one's own work often looks even better in print—it also serves to affirm the commitment we've made to the academic profession (the "mountain" we "climb" everyday) and to legitimize the many days and long hours involved in crafting the work. Most importantly, this ritual is a sure-fire way to generate new ideas about one's own line of research and areas of writing. By reading the work in print as a stranger might, we are often able to see it from a fresh angle, make new connections to the field, generate several new questions, and even outline a follow-up research design or book idea. Of course, we never go on these brief contemplative ventures without paper and pen handy.

Deliberate contemplation is an essential ingredient in the long-term health and productivity of most academics. But don't get mired in contemplation to the point of obsessive compulsiveness, and never let contemplation serve as an excuse to avoid writing. Contemplation on one's writing life and impact on the field fits nicely in-between those sacrosanct writing blocks!

5

KNOW WHEN TO COLLABORATE
AND WHEN TO CUT LOSSES

In this chapter we discuss the important message of knowing when to collaborate and when to cut your losses and leave a project or writing group. For one thing, find supportive colleagues and constructive editors in the effort to support your writing growth, and join groups and networks focused on academic development and scholarly productivity. For another thing, collaborate often but selectively by forming genuine writing partnerships that facilitate production of your scholarship; even productive scholars who work alone can experience greater productivity from synergistic writing relationships. Additionally, avoid the hard lessons learned about not clarifying expectations before agreeing to collaborate, and compel all involved to be intentionally explicit about these. Also, carefully structure the collaboration with respect to such pivotal issues as order of authorship and expectations with respect to not only the writing but also the revising of the work and communications with editors. Know when to cash out or walk away from a project—sometimes we have no choice—but learn from your mistakes and avoid repeating them.

28   FIND SUPPORTIVE COLLEAGUES AND
CRITICAL EDITORS

Writing can be a lonely endeavor. The self-discipline, tenacity, and sometimes monastic commitment to the task at hand can be trying and even overwhelming for the best of us. Although there will be plenty of hours and days when we need to do the work alone, it is nearly always helpful to enjoy the steady back-up of a writing support network—a cast of characters who support and encourage our writing. Some of these colleagues will be coauthors but others may be scholars in different disciplines, friends, or even relatives who, in addition to their own writing, inspire or critique our ideas and bolster our writing motivation and efficacy without even doing any writing with us. No matter its size, parameters, or criteria for membership, we encourage you to deliberately foster a supportive writing network.

Supportive colleagues can be found in many places but are most often faculty members with whom you interact frequently. These may be other junior professors or senior faculty in your department or around the larger campus. Quite often, brand new assistant professors are most motivated to seek out and reciprocate assistance and support with writing. At times, a department, school, or even the larger university will establish and promote weekly or monthly writing groups or teams— often specifically targeting untenured faculty. These are excellent opportunities to meet regularly with other fledgling scholars and/or writing guides, share ideas and concerns, and offer reciprocal constructive feedback and moral support. At times, new faculty may be formally assigned to a writing cohort or team in hopes of spurring early scholarly activity. Regardless, do not wait until you have writing projects up and running before you join or even create a highly viable working group that satisfies your goals.

In one of our departments, a regular colloquium brings together all faculty for the purpose of collegial support for personal scholarship. Once a year, each professor takes a turn presenting his or her latest paper, followed by a period of open brainstorming about the topic, constructive feedback, and recommendations for improvement and support. Although it may feel like a "hassle" to get one's material ready to present to colleagues, the process is often a boon in terms of forcing us to sharpen our latest work—this duty to present our writing often ends up being the impetus to get a manuscript ready for submission to a journal. It is also a great opportunity to garner new insights about possible problems or necessary modifications to the piece. Frankly, it is a rewarding experience characterized by collegial reinforcement of our works-in-progress that serves to enhance the quality of each piece presented. If such a writing group or faculty colloquium is not in place in your department or college, why not take the initiative for getting it off the ground? Volunteer to go first and set the tone by being prepared and receptive to feedback. If there is not a host of other colleagues in your institution who could also use this kind of encouragement and motivational push, your institution may place less emphasis on research and publication than most.

In addition to formal groups, a writing support constellation might include individual colleagues—either in your department or across campus, established mentors in your discipline, or even supportive services for new faculty offered by professional organizations. Among individual colleagues, look for those friends and confidants you enjoyed in graduate school, colleagues in your department with whom you instantly "hit it off," or even friends and acquaintances outside of academe who happen to write themselves or who take an interest in your work. When a colleague or friend proves to be an especially capable and constructive reviewer of your work, foster that connection, return the favor if he or she too could use support with writing, and let them know you appreciate the help. When the context is conducive, set up regular (or spontaneous) meeting times with these valuable colleagues and over beverages or a meal share your recent ideas, solicit feedback regarding manuscripts you've given them to read, and make these opportunities not only enjoyable and helpful but also, to the extent possible over time, mutually beneficial.

This brings us to an important point about seeking out and retaining supportive colleagues. A well-constructed writing network should offer two salient functions as you work to get the writing done. First, supportive colleagues and friends should offer emotional encouragement. If you *feel* good about yourself and motivated to write more and more often after interacting with these individuals, you've probably tapped the right people as far as synergy goes. Although many academics are introverted by nature, few are full-fledged islands; nearly all of us benefit, and in ways not always clear at the time, from ardent supporters and trustworthy friends. Make sure that the inner circle in your own writing network is reliably and unconditionally encouraging—even when delivering tough feedback. Second, good writing colleagues should provide excellent practical and technical advice. Only rare colleagues will copyedit your work unless you reciprocate, so be sure to avoid imposing. If you could use assistance at the more technical level of writing, solicit support from professional proofreaders and copyeditors, who typically charge an hourly rate. But within your writing circle, seek out those supporters who know the writing enterprise and are both willing and eager to show you how to write more accurately, more effectively, and more professionally. Often times, they will want to direct you to something written that can serve as a guide rather than to actually spend the time "penning" changes on your work. If they are genuinely supportive, it will be easier to take advantage of this technical assistance, whatever the form.

Here is one more thing to consider. If there are people in your current network, or life more generally, who are the antithesis of supportive, we must ask: Why are you wasting your time and energy with them? Prolific writing is hard enough without having to contend with chronic naysayers, sabotaging colleagues, or even family and friends who disparage your commitment to scholarship. Life is short and the time to tenure and promotion are shorter. Curtail contact with corrosive critics (but be sure there are not some nuggets of truth in their comments), jettison colleagues or writing support groups when meetings with them amount to little more than gripe or counseling sessions, and when a significant other or even a partner cannot support your writing, seriously ask why. Are you ignoring balance and neglecting relationship obligations? Is relationship counseling needed? Can you continue in a relationship in which your partner shows no regard for something so central to the heart of your vocation? These are hard questions but worth asking early on even if they take time away from your productivity because, after all, core relational problems have a way of resurrecting themselves; you'll need to take sanctuary in a place that's conducive to your well-being if you are to write.

Seek supportive and constructively critical colleagues, friends, and professionals. Partake in encouraging writing groups and partnerships with other professors and writers. But whatever you do, don't mistake time spent in these supportive endeavors with writing productivity. While outstanding support will fuel and hone your writing, it will neither expedite the writing nor absolve you of the duty to lock your door and put nose to grindstone. There is a grave distinction between talking about the process of building a home and actually doing the work, metaphorically speaking. Receive writing support gratefully, return the favor reliably, and then work relentlessly!

29   COLLABORATE OFTEN BUT SELECTIVELY

Here is a consistent similarity among prolific academics: They create writing/authorship networks or multi-author teams that facilitate production of far more scholarship than they could possibly have produced alone. We refer here to genuine writing partnerships; more than just supportive colleagues, these are our coauthors and (hopefully) long-term cocreators of streams of consistent publication. Even when a scholar is quite effective and productive working alone, entering into a synergistic writing pair or team often allows the academic to cover considerably more ground. And even when you continue to write solo pieces, it may require surprisingly little time or modest effort to simultaneously contribute to one or two team products. Such collaboration may allow you to participate in parallel projects, or maybe contribute to a different area of study altogether. Here is a fact: For most of us, joining with the right coauthors is destined to accelerate our rate of publication and, hopefully, deepen our insight and broaden our knowledge base, and, importantly, increase our enjoyment of what is otherwise very hard work.

When we examine the vitae of highly productive academics we generally notice a track record of solo publications in their areas of specialty as well as numerous streams of multi-authored studies that reflect their collaborations with talented graduate students and colleagues. (Some productive writers publish strictly on their own or only with others.) Sometimes these collaborations are limited to one publication—a common scenario for anyone who chairs a dissertation and publishes with his or her students. In other instances, there is a lengthy list of presentations and publications with the same coauthor or group. Quite often the order of authorship changes as different ideas for articles emerge and members of the team take turns as the lead. In many cases the focus of these products is one's own area(s) of expertise. But in other instances, the topics are idiosyncratic deviations from the primary area of emphasis— perhaps reflecting an interest of a colleague who happened to intrigue us with an errant idea, or a short-term dalliance in a new research area. For example, several years ago, one of us became interested in self-help materials for clinical use and collaborated with a colleague in writing two articles. While the collaboration was enjoyable and made the writing expeditious, we have never revisited the topic. While this side road proved to be nothing but a fascinating cul-de-sac, these sidelight foci sometimes become long-term—if infrequent—areas of scholarly interest.

Beyond sheer acceleration of your productivity as a scholar, there is another sound reason for carefully selecting coauthors and collaborators over the course of your scholarly career: Collaborators tend to become lifelong friends. In our own case, strolling down memory lane in the form of glancing at the lines of our vitae is a nostalgic experience. The names that leap off the pages over the years amount to a "who's who" of our life stories. Our coauthors include favorite students, good colleagues, and some of our best friends, as well as, let's face it, hard-learned mistakes that may have changed how we think about and select collaborators. What shows up merely as a list of publications on the printed page actually conjures reminiscences of rich, or at least educational, collaborative experiences, sometimes stretching over many years. It is certainly true that excellent collaborative relationships can thwart loneliness— something all too common in the writing life—and imbue the entire process of research and writing with a sense of synergistic excitement and creative meaning. Unless you are a rather extreme introvert always content in solitary pursuit of your work, we urge you to give serious thought to joining or creating promising scholarly networks—especially when you find prolific writers in your area of interest who are responsive to colearning endeavors.

So, how should you go about finding the right coauthors for you? This is a critically important challenge. Selecting scholarly collaborators should be just as deliberate as choosing the right mate or the right friends—remember: The best collaborators can become career-long coauthors. Several factors contribute to both the match and the probable outcomes of your work together. Some of the most important of these include personality features, collegiality, work ethic, writing ability, and creativity. In our experience, the best coauthors have been punctual in correspondence, assiduous about meeting writing deadlines, smart and creative, efficient when it comes to churning out pages, and most important, motivating and energizing, even fun to be around. Great collaborators are also clear communicators, open about their preferences and concerns, and endowed with a good sense of humor. And they express appreciation for the efforts of their coauthors, not taking for granted their special skills and talents or especially how they may have had to put in extra time to complete a particular task, such as communication with a publisher or analysis of a data set. Finally, you should be certain to seek out evidence of fair-mindedness in any prospective coauthor. Nothing sours a partnership faster than a tendency to be self-focused and unfair. Find colleagues who seem just as concerned about your interests as their own and who are prepared to negotiate coauthorship terms from the outset and, if necessary, to reassess them.

Good collaborations—including the creation of writing teams—often begin through reputation, exposure, and interaction. This commonly occurs around campus or at professional meetings where conversations about shared interests, colloquia presentations, or scholarly panels lead to exciting collaborative possibilities. However, it is not necessary to meet an exemplary collaborator in person before commencing work. We serve as a shining example of this postmodern reality.

When I (Brad) began thinking about a short guide on writing geared to higher education faculty, I wondered about writing the book with a colleague—someone who also liked to write and who could bring another perspective to the work. And then a light went on. A fellow scholar in the area of mentoring relationships, the editor of a journal (*Mentoring & Tutoring*) in which I had recently published an article, and a prolific writer in her own right came immediately to mind. Although I had never met Carol in person (and to this day have not), I knew from significant correspondence, from reading her work, and from reviewing her vita in the context of writing a review for one of her many books, that Carol was a truly prolific academic. I knew she was also a kind, witty, and creative person with a work ethic that rivaled my own. In spite of our lack of personal acquaintance, I knew Carol would be a stellar coauthor. Carol responded to the idea of a collaborative book with just the sort of competence, excitement, and intensity I have come to expect from her and so we got to work and have never looked back. We have come to experience each other as friends and phenomenal colleagues and approach our writing relationship from a shared sense of respect.

Synergy builds synergy, and so, just as I (Brad) had launched the idea for the book, Carol had recently done the same with a journal article on tensions involving accountability and democracy in the lives of school leaders. We wrote that piece and published it while writing this book and simultaneously preparing a number of additional projects, both with each other and separately with other coauthors, moving around our various pots on the stove while trying to help each other out and not get in each others' way!

Although writing partnerships are a must for thesis-and-dissertation supervisors, and for most professors interested in accelerating their work, there are some sobering cautions to heed before racing headlong into these arrangements. First, the number of students and colleagues who are either unreliable when it comes to getting the work done or just plain lousy at writing is indeed mind-boggling. We say this not to disparage novice writers or our own colleagues but merely to expose the truth. Excellent writing—and the work often required to achieve a level of scholarly excellence—is uncommon. There are legions of good students and solid college professors who simply lack the passion, interest, drive, collegial disposition, or facility with words needed to excel at academic writing. Be careful about the decisions and investments you make: Wade in slowly to coauthored and multi-authored projects. Carefully evaluate potential collaborators' publishing records and degree of success, interpersonal strengths and weaknesses, and styles of work. If working with a graduate student, be realistic about his or her capacity to deliver usable material, and when working with a faculty colleague, consider a smaller "pilot" project before making a larger commitment to a time-consuming and risky project.

Obviously, some risks are clearly associated with writing partnerships. But when you are intentional about the match and discover a worthy collaborator, the potential personal and professional benefits far outweigh the risks. Take a gamble today but be sure it is a calculated risk: Be as informed as possible about the writing partners and projects you choose.

30 CAREFULLY STRUCTURE COLLABORATIVE PROJECTS

Too many scholars learn the hard way to be intentionally explicit about expectations before agreeing to collaborate. Prolific scholars learn early on that participation in coauthored works can accelerate productivity only *if* one sees eye-to-eye with collaborators and only *when* collaborators are conscientious and clear about expectations. In order to prevent any of the various misunderstandings that can easily thwart or even doom coauthored products, it is incumbent upon you to take the lead in clarifying and concretizing expectations and parameters.

Like solid homes, good writing partnerships begin with careful planning and construction that follow an approved blueprint. As a busy professor with precious little time for bad scholarly investments, you must thoughtfully select your coauthors (see the previous section) and then take initiative to craft shared expectations upfront. A number of important issues must be clarified at the start in order to avoid, to the extent humanly possibly, disappointment or even outright anger later on. First, what are the necessary deadlines en route to completing the project, and can each author agree to meet them? This is crucial. We know of no other issue that causes so much angst in the world of academic collaboration than that of missed timelines. Agreeing to produce a section of an article, a book chapter, or a portion of a coauthored book must be considered a sacred duty. It is not only your own scholarly success that hangs in the balance but that of other colleagues as well.

Avoid telling yourself a Hollywood story about the coauthoring relationship—none is perfect because each is subjected to the fallacies and idiosyncrasies of being human. It is easy early in any collaboration to see a coauthor through rose-colored lenses. Social psychologists call this the *halo effect*—making a broad positive assessment of a colleague's skills, capacities, and personality traits on the basis of one or two positive features (e.g., employment at a prestigious institution, attractiveness, warm conversational style). Of course, such positive factors as these may have nothing at all to do with writing acumen or fair-minded collegiality. So be cautious as you enter in and discuss possible problems and solutions early on.

By all means, converse about both intermediate and final deadlines and make decisions ahead of time involving the rights and protections of authors. For example, should a collaborator be late with his or her section, do the remaining authors have the right to produce this part on their own or, alternatively, to seek another collaborator? Do all agree in advance that the tardy colleague will be dropped as a coauthor from the project?

Of course, punctuality leads to another issue that demands explication whenever a joint project is undertaken: Order of authorship. Here is a subject that causes a great deal of angst and conflict in the halls of academe, not to mention more than a few legal and ethical complaints between professors who may have once been good friends. Decide, then, who will be the first author listed? What will be the specific order of authorship if more than two are involved? What circumstances or occurrences along the way would be cause to change authorship order and what will the process be for making this determination as early as possible? If more than one publication should stem from the current data set or writing team, will order of authorship rotate? What about subsequent conference presentations or books that spin off from the current work? As you can see, it is critical that authorship order be made crystal clear at the start and revisited as often as needed to avoid ill will or hurt feelings. And don't forget to be just as explicit in your negotiations when supervising the work of a graduate student. It's essential that ethical guidelines be followed and cultural norms understood (e.g., graduate students should generally be first author of collaborative works leading to or emanating from their dissertations).

Other expectations demanding clarification early on in the formation of any writing partnership include writing style, anticipated frequency of contact or consultation, and preferred methods of transferring drafts back and forth (e.g., over the Internet, possibly using the track changes function in Word, through the postal service, by fax). Some additional expectations involve anticipated number and outlets for scholarly products, issues pertaining to ownership of copyrighted material, and whether decisions about manuscript content and style will always be democratic or assigned to the first author. Who on the team will articulate a conceptual framework, review the literature, collect and analyze data, and ultimately pen the final draft of the manuscript? And later on, should a decision letter arrive from the editor requesting a thorough rewrite of the paper followed by resubmission, whose responsibility will it be to take the lead on (or even to tackle solo) the revision? The list goes on.

Here is another reason to clarify expectations early on. All of us are prone to become so excited about a new project or so flattered by an invitation to coauthor—especially if a luminary in the field extends the offer—that we can say *yes* too quickly, perhaps without taking honest stock of our current commitments. Before we know it, we have gotten in too deep and stand to forfeit in a way that might both disappoint our colleagues and blight our reputation as collaborators. A process of clarifying expectations offers an inherent "cooling off" period during which a potential contributor is encouraged to honestly assess his or her ability to come through with quality work and on time.

If it is not already apparent, defining expectations adequately requires appropriate boldness and assertiveness as well as thorough knowledge of self. Only the self-acquainted and transparent scholar can let new collaborators know what he or she expects, likes, and prefers with regard to the writing relationship and what pitfalls must be steadfastly avoided. Good collaborators know their relative strengths and weaknesses and seek coauthors who can tolerate their foibles while bolstering the weaker areas. Do you have pet peeves when it comes to writing with others? Our own list of examples includes tardiness, poor-quality contributions, and a negative, obstructionist attitude. If so, be sure that coauthors know about them upfront.

Some prolific scholars are so careful about clarifying expectations that they even draft contracts and place responsibilities and timelines in writing. Think of a writing contract as a sort of prenuptial agreement for scholarly collaborators. Contracts offer the benefit of allowing participants to think carefully about mutual expectations while negotiating roles, timelines, and other critical matters. They also offer a potent impetus to follow-through. But there is a downside to importing such formal tools into a collegial scholarly relationship. A contract can paradoxically diminish intrinsic interest, collegial altruism, and the very spontaneity that often make such collaborations delightful in the first place.

In our experience, formal clarification of role expectations and deadlines—whether in writing or not—is profoundly valuable. This proves indispensable in fledgling collaborations and less necessary as a writing duo or team develops a track record rooted in trust, synergy, and success. But flexibility is also an essential ingredient in good collaboration and, it goes without saying that sacrifices will have to be made in other areas of your life in order to sustain the work and relationship. Adhere to deadlines whenever humanly possible, expect your collaborators to do the same, and when necessary (which is often, in our experience!), show grace and flexibility, even when you have to reassess collaboration with a delinquent colleague. Know what qualities and competencies you expect your collaborators to embody and find out what they, in turn, expect from theirs, and with this knowledge, seek to create good writing matches.

31   KNOW WHEN TO CASH OUT

Sometimes, it is necessary to walk away from a scholarly project—even one in which you have invested considerable time. There can be many reasons for this. In the nomenclature of writing projects, we hope that most of your work will fall into such positive categories of experience as "grand success," "noteworthy achievement," or at least "solid contribution to the literature." Yet there are outcomes at the other end of the project spectrum that can be labeled "stinker," "dead on arrival," and so forth. Anyone who writes will admit to being involved with at least a few projects that can be deemed failures—sometimes these are individual flops and sometimes failed group efforts. One secret to success as a prolific writer is the ability to diagnose potentially dead-end projects early on and take appropriate action to avoid them altogether or at least cut them loose at the first opportunity.

Let's face it, every writing project, regardless of the level of commitment and intensity, will require an investment on your part. A professor's time, energy, and resources are precious commodities and each new article, chapter, or book idea requires varying degrees of personal investment. When we as academics carefully consider our resources and the likely return on specific projects, we often make wise investment decisions. But even with impeccable planning, things can change in your life, in those of colleagues, or in the area of your scholarly focus; either suddenly or gradually, evidence accumulates that your current project is doomed—or at least unlikely to reap the expected or perhaps even any returns. It is also true that the picture of failure can vary considerably with scholarly experience. Prolific academics often judge their major projects a failure if only one solid article has resulted, whereas new scholars may feel that this kind of return signifies success.

Here are some common indicators that you should reconsider investment in a writing project. While no single indicator may always necessitate walking away, each should serve as a glaring red flag:

1. An Institutional Review Board (IRB) denies access to data collection essential to the work at hand

2. An IRB or another official gate keeping body refuses to approve an innovative new procedure or a research design indispensable to the work
3. A collaborator with access to critical data or literature never follows through
4. Results from a pilot study or analysis of some early data indicate that your approach or theory is problematic and possibly invalid
5. A key coauthor is clearly unreliable or otherwise very difficult to work with
6. Editors and reviewers reject the work or idea outright—perhaps pointing out fatal and indefensible flaws in the design or theory
7. Trusted colleagues or an administrative head cautions that the work is unlikely to bolster your case for promotion and tenure
8. The project has begun to seriously compromise your health and well being

In each case, the writing may be on the wall, so to speak; continued investment of resources in an idea constrained by any such circumstances may be a colossal waste of time and may even work at cross purposes with your goal of establishing a solid resume of scholarly work.

Our cautionary words and advice apply to bad collaborators, not just to bad ideas. We have emphasized in different parts of this book that choosing writing partners must be done carefully and deliberately. But there will always be some false positives that sneak through your selection grid. When it becomes apparent that a colleague is chronically late, unreliable, prone to low quality work, or perhaps caustic and hard to communicate with, by all means, be honest about the unfortunate circumstances in which you find yourself—take a deep breath, cut your losses, and move on! And learn from your mistakes: Do your best to avoid similar circumstances and collaborators in the future.

Here is one caveat when it comes to cashing out and dropping scholarly "duds:" Sometimes, deciding when to stay the course or to pull out instead is not an easy challenge. For instance, you may have devoted substantial time to a project only to have an editor inform you that a thorough and complete rewrite and hence resubmission will be required. One of us spent several months writing a lengthy review article that summarized decades worth of research on a specific assessment issue. What appeared to be an interesting topic soon turned laborious and onerous. Then, the journal editor requested revisions that were not only substantial but also vague. The prospect of continuing this work was both daunting and depressing; but so many hours had been invested, and the probability of ultimately having the article accepted for publication so probable, that the author decided to stay the course, endure the pain, and get the revisions completed. After two rounds of more manageable revisions the article was finally accepted for publication.

Were this author (Brad) to live his academic life over again, he would not choose to write that particular article. But in retrospect, he is glad that he saw this project through to fruition, as has Carol in similar arduous circumstances. And yet, both of us have also walked away from projects that quickly proved untenable—even after devoting some important time and energy to getting them off the ground. In nearly every case, our instinct to abandon at the time proved wise. In other cases such projects have not been abandoned, turning to rust in our filing cabinets; in some instances, they have been resurrected into more viable bodies of work and hence accepted for publication either as articles or book chapters. Over time, wisdom born of experience will help you discern when to persevere and when to cash out.

In a classic country song, Kenny Rogers advises listeners to "know when to hold 'em, know when to fold 'em; know when to walk away, and know when to run." To become prolific, you must master the art of detecting writing project stinkers early on and then gracefully but expeditiously dropping them like hot potatoes. You must also learn to distinguish between stinkers that should be dropped altogether and potentially good works for which you should stay the course. Like quicksand, poorly conceived ideas, flawed designs, or bad collaborators can pull you down and derail productivity; none of us can afford costly distractions for which the scholarly price is loss of precious time and energy. So stay alert—and know when to cash out.

6

PRACTICE SYSTEMATIC
WRITING FROM
START TO FINISH

In this section we focus on a number of pragmatic issues related to writing. We begin with the importance of cleaning your desk and filing your work, and move to that of developing a sound writing system. In both instances we share old-fashioned and computerized strategies for getting the work underway. With respect to sound writing systems, we refer to both linear and organic planning strategies that work well in organizing major scholarly projects. In order to help propel publishing success, we advocate for choosing the journal (or publisher) early on. By shaping the manuscript to the requirements of specific journals or publishing houses, you should experience higher initial success. We also recommend that you give focus and legitimacy to your work by deciding on your title early. Also, consider working on one manuscript at a time to its completion, which will enable you to learn the challenging and complex skills that go into developing a manuscript for publication review. Practice the art of generating multiple products when possible: Write smart by conceptualizing a program or string of publications on a topic that will add to the volume of your accomplishments. Related to this, write programmatically and maintain a focus by establishing a scholarly niche; produce works that are relevant to your scholarly agenda and related in some way. Pick the low-hanging fruit first, meaning get the easiest work done first so that your works will move more rapidly into and out of the publishing cue. Also, overestimate time to completion so that you will meet publishing deadlines and avoid adding stress to your life. Last but not least, we discuss how quality matters, but so does quantity; you will want to publish with regularity and with peer-reviewed presses—don't assume any one publication will be important enough to guarantee tenure.

32   CLEAN YOUR DESK AND FILE YOUR WORK

Organization in writing enhances productivity, plain and simple. It is often the case that poor organization inhibits productivity; it may even inhibit personal well-being. The physical aspects of your writing environment have everything to do with your preparedness for the task. An office in disarray (and there are many of these in the halls of academe) may be reflective of internal disorganization or habitual procrastination. Distracting piles or the inability to quickly locate crucial resources can easily stymie writing. One of us knows a tenured professor who is notorious for the shocking state of her office—literally, no one can enter because of the floor-to-ceiling paper stacks, and no research projects are ever completed because only pieces of each "lost city" are ever found. Don't get us wrong, many scholarly laureates work expediently in offices resembling trash heaps, but these are the exceptions.

All things being equal, you would do well to clear your primary workspace of stacks and clutter. File all of your resources and your own works-in-progress neatly and expeditiously. If you wonder how organized your writing space is, consider the *twister test*. If a small windstorm were to pass through your office tomorrow, how long would it take you to be ready to write again? If the answer is more than ten minutes, get busy filing. Spend some time filing every day.

That being said, don't file away your writing deadlines! Post these prominently so that none is missed. It is not enough to keep such information tucked away in a file or stored "in memory." You cannot expect to remember due dates with so much going on all of the time. Highlight in your calendar critical dates and have a system somewhere on your desk for doing the same—a simple post-it can work just fine. Be your own best secretary.

Here's an organizational tip that should stimulate your productivity: Keep your current writing files in *full view* at all times so that you will remember your priority commitment as you get knocks at the door, check e-mail, go out to lunch, get lost in daydreams, and so forth. Color-coded accordion folders labeled with project titles are a good old-fashioned idea, as are corresponding computer desktop folders containing the same critical information. Be especially mindful of that precious raw data that only exist in hard copy; consider scanning handwritten, completed surveys and other original documents into computer files so that you will have duplicates. Some writers like to use transparent bins for organizing their projects so that bulky materials can be easily identified, accommodated, and trans-ported. If you need more (or better) ideas, talk to the produc-tive scholars you know to see what systems they use; adopt and improvise as you see fit. You can also visit your nearest office supply store (or surf the Web) to garner the latest ideas for organization and storage.

As you prepare for tenure review, the need for excellent systems of organization becomes increasingly apparent. Consider working toward that reality today. While tenure-earning, organize your filing cabinet with separate drawers devoted to research, teaching, and service. Or, secure three large bins with handles, and devote one to research productivity, the second to teaching, and the third to service. You can create "mirror" files on your desktop. Tenure-and-promotion committees as well as future employers will require that your dossier be submitted in either hard copy or electronic form; regardless, the research/ teaching/service organizational system fits well with most institutions' expectations for protocol.

Keep your folders on your thumbdrive and on an up-to-date CD ROM. If you are coauthoring with someone else or a team of collaborators, be sure to always have all manuscript versions under your control. Not all writing partners are vigilant about being well organized so it's best not to expect this—assume responsibility for master files and revisions. Avoid time-wasters and mini-disasters from occurring wherein the latest version of a paper cannot be located.

Increasingly, academic writers are "toss[ing] out the index cards" in favor of "computer programs that take on the tedious chore of crafting footnotes and bibliographies," so you, too, may want to think about making this change (Kiernan, 2006, A29). Bibliographic software will organize your sources into easy-to-use databases that not only correctly format references, footnotes, and endnotes but also convert these into the various formatting styles required by editors and publishers. Electronic information systems such as EndNote and RefWorks have been praised by professors and students alike. Those interviewed for the *Chronicle of Higher Education* say that these systems make the compilation and formatting of multiple sources practical and relatively stress-free (Kiernan, 2006). At a minimum, you may want to create a file that contains all of your bibliographic sources so that you can at least copy-and-paste at will.

If you were, hypothetically speaking, to lose your work office to a natural disaster tomorrow, what would you be left with? Would you be fortunate enough to have your latest files at home or in another safe place? Always keep two complete sets of up-to-date materials on file, one at home, and the other at the office. We know that this sounds like extra work, because it is, but this practice can also save you in the end. By maintaining a tenure-and-promotion backup system at home containing copies of all key documents and drafts related to teaching, research, and service, you will be protected from acts of nature and overzealous campus janitors who occasionally mistake files or bins for recycling! In the summer of 2004 while teaching full-time, Carol's Florida home was struck by lightning; the author's computer, along with loads of other electrical equipment, fried. Luckily, the scholarly disaster that could have compounded the natural one was averted. One of the firefighters who had extinguished the billowing smoke nodded knowingly at the precious object being cradled—not a photograph, diary, or jewelry but the author's thumbdrive containing all computer files. The writing life saved.

33 DEVELOP A SOUND WRITING SYSTEM

Most prolific writers adopt and hone an idiosyncratic but effective strategy for tackling the tasks or steps in the writing process. Like a Rorschach test, authors' organizational strategies and habits come through in the systems they develop for writing. We have talked with many prolific scholars to learn about their writing systems. A consistent habit among these scholars is the predilection toward brainstorming individually or with a colleague or student before putting anything on paper—they formulate and refine their ideas to the extent possible early on; they clearly articulate the big picture. This preliminary work helps maintain a stringent focus in subsequent stages of the project; systematic visioning allows the writer to avoid pursuing irrelevant—though tempting—side issues that often consume precious time and energy.

While some productive scholars use the old-fashioned strategy of writing out their ideas longhand on legal pads, with scratchouts identifying changes, others develop their ideas right on their laptops or desktops. Some computer-oriented individuals are almost completely paperless. We also know writers who dictate their ideas into an audio/digital recorder, another strategy not only for brainstorming ideas but also for developing outlines. Outlines, like ideas and entire papers, can be developed electronically or on paper. While some writers, like artists, produce many increasingly refined sketches before doing the actual writing, others do not—this depends in part on the extent to which they have already worked out the key ideas.

Some academics write from a detailed plan, or at least an outline or series of sketches, while others are more bare bone, preferring to see what emerges organically and spontaneously. For example, one of us uses a more linear planning strategy in our writing than the other, so we developed a detailed, step-by-step outline for the prospectus and later for the book itself. We knew the content of each chapter and section before we proceeded with the writing. For each section, we wrote a paragraph describing it and for each chapter we prepared an overview statement. After we could see the big picture emerge, we were free to move around the pieces until all of the parts fit together; finally, we split up the task, each of us taking responsibility for drafting half of the book, with the supporting author doing the rewriting and the initial author doing the revising. Of course, additional secrets dawned on us during the act of writing and ongoing brainstorming via e-mail—we stayed open to the new ideas and made room for them in our manuscript.

Just as individual writers have systemic writing approaches, so too do coauthors and writing teams. We have shared the writing system we used for this book project. As another example, an outrageously prolific scholar we know who heads an educational center has a different system—he alone does the conceptualization work for the various coauthored writing projects that he leads. Project coordinators and faculty researchers provide him with the basic information he needs to write up the ideas and put them in finished form. His coauthors admire his ability to put onto paper, with apparent ease, impressive conceptual frameworks and powerful abstractions. The sound writing system modeled in this case relies upon the strengths of each contributor, some better at brainstorming core ideas, others better at summarizing the relevant literature, still others better at drafting and polishing ideas, and so forth.

Another similarly prolific writer, known for his outstanding organization and discipline, produces proposals for conferences that are highly unusual—the research is already done and the paper written *before* he writes the proposal. The singular focus this individual maintains is seen as highly unusual because, unlike most scholars, his writing system is so well organized he knows one or more years in advance what he will be working on. The highly predictable writing schedule he maintains every day includes a careful account of plans and tasks accomplished, all recorded on index cards.

So far, we have taken a macro approach to conceptualizing writing systems. But what about a systematic approach to a single scholarly project? Here's a common approach that you might consider when writing a scholarly article, book, or another major work:

1. Conceptualize the title and scope of the paper
2. Collect and analyze any data to be included
3. Collect published literature on the topic
4. Read through the literature, making notes of key ideas or quotations
5. Develop a detailed outline of the manuscript, using numbers to denote key sections and subsections (e.g., 1a, 1b, 2a)
6. Return to your notes and number key points accordingly
7. Begin writing by collecting every card and paper with "1a" in the margin spread them out on your desk, and start in
8. When finished with section 1a, proceed to the next section and so on
9. When done with a first draft, print it out, and immediately begin to revise.

This methodical approach has served us well in various writing projects over the years. It offers a clear method for breaking down a seemingly monumental task into clear steps and a cogent, systematic process. As your own writing career matures, you will undoubtedly arrive at a system that works for you. In the end, we are pragmatists; when an approach to conceptualizing, organizing, and carrying out the writing enterprise works for you, go with it!

34 CHOOSE THE JOURNAL (OR PUBLISHER) FIRST

Do you want to know how to save gargantuan quantities of time during the process of publishing a scholarly manuscript? Select an appropriate outlet for your work early on. In fact, once the data are collected, the idea for an article formulated, or the book framework conceptualized, choosing a journal or publisher should precede starting the actual writing. By targeting the manuscript's tone, style, length, and contents to the requirements of a specific journal or publisher, you are radically increasing the chances for initial success. You are also reducing costs in terms of the time involved in resubmitting the manuscript for major structural revisions or, if rejected, to other journals. As advised in a later chapter on publishing, closely adhere to the journal's guidelines for authors—if a specific type of formatting is required, adopt it and do so consistently. Over the years, we have discovered that deciding on a journal usually occurs during the same ponderous jog or over the same cup of tea that served to generate the article title and outline. Once the article's rough outline, title, and likely publishing outlet take form, we are able to tailor our work to the journal's style and specifications.

Be sure to access issues and read articles published in your targeted publication so that you will become familiar with the publication's scope, philosophy, style, and contents. Editors can readily discern which authors of submitted manuscripts are familiar with their publication. An impression will be created rather quickly about the potential "worthiness" of your work, so carefully select the journal and follow its guidelines; where relevant, consider situating your piece within the context of the journal's philosophy or orientation and even citing the works relevant to your own. Keep in mind that vigilance in selecting the most appropriate outlet will save you and the editor/ publisher a significant amount of valuable time.

Regarding the selection of a journal at the outset, you should most definitely learn what the rejection (or acceptance) rate is before making your determination. Such statistics are sometimes made available in various places on the Internet; however, because journals rarely publicize their acceptance rates, you can either ask the editor (or assistant) before deciding or consult an official source, notably *Cabell's Directory*, which is accessible online (http://www.cabells.com). Research the journals in your field by using this official source or one like it; however, if the journal you're interested in is relatively new or nonmainstream it will not be listed in any publication guides. The publishers of the official directories use criteria, such as citation and circulation rates, for making decisions about which journals will be listed.

Regarding *Cabell's*, each journal entry includes the "editor's name, address, phone, fax, email and web address, manuscript guidelines; acceptance rate, review type, process, and time; number of reviewers; circulation and price; and type of readership." The directory index classifies "journals by different topic areas and provides information on type of review, number of external reviewers and acceptance rate." Where this information does not appear in an official guide, feel free to contact journal editors or their staff: Ask not only about acceptance rates but also the turnaround time for review and possibly how many months it takes before a work that has been accepted appears in published form.

If seeking a journal that is prestigious, even top-tier in your field, you will want to identify one that has a low acceptance rate of approximately 10 percent or less (but ask productive colleagues for clarification relative to your discipline). Expect to experience a longer review period and, at best, "accept with major modifications" on the first, second, or even third round of reviews. Such journals bring out the obsessive-compulsive or competitive personality within many of us. On the other hand, journals that have a 25 percent acceptance rate are respectable within most academic circles. The prolific scholars we know have had a significant impact by publishing in practitioner journals (with higher acceptance rates) in addition to leading academic journals (with lower acceptance rates). Such national-level practitioner journals usually disseminate widely and have many readers, whereas prestigious journals tend to have modest circulation and hence modest readership and citation. However, those "lighthouse" or leading academic journals in which the "big names" publish can also have an impressive distribution, as in the case of the top-tier journals in our own professions, the American Psychological Association's *American Psychologist*, and the American Educational Research Association's *Educational Researcher*.

Of course, the same concerns are present when seeking a book publisher. While some academic publishers—including many university presses—may be known for carefully scrutinizing and vetting scholarly proposals, these publishers may have a relatively narrow impact in terms of marketing and circulation of your work. On the other hand, trade publishers offer the advantage of much broader attention to your work and perhaps extensive marketing resources. On the down side, trade publishers may push for a more reader-friendly and less scholarly version of your work. The salient point is that the publication outlet will necessarily shape your writing. For this reason, we recommend never writing more than a book prospectus and one or two chapters of the book before seeking a publisher and signing a contract.

Carefully weigh the benefits and drawbacks of each of the journals in your discipline that could potentially serve as good venues for your work. Remember, it is the pattern of publication, not any one particular piece, that is important for gaining tenure and contributing to your impact and success as a scholar. Whether you decide to target exclusively top-tier journals or whether you disseminate your scholarship more broadly, we return to the primary point of this section: For each journal article or book you write, select your outlet early on.

35 WRITE YOUR TITLE EARLY

After selecting the outlet (or publisher, in the case of a book), write your title. Take time with this task. Informing your search for the right title are the key concepts in your piece: prevailing norms in the publications you are reading—especially the one that will receive your material for review—and your own creative muse. The title should be substantive and possibly laced with humor or irony. Of course, it should also thoroughly capture the gist of your contribution. Select concise words that give your work focus and serve as a touchstone for crafting the manuscript; a good title should keep you on track and make your writing more coherent. It also communicates a promise to yourself that you will want to uphold. Try your title on trusted colleagues for feedback and hone accordingly. Expect your title to change as you engage in the creative process of writing and as your thinking becomes clarified. Remain open to both nuanced alterations and thoroughgoing revisions of the title as you work.

All of these processes held true during the time we spent on developing our own book title. It underwent numerous changes before its current rendition—we wanted to love it, not just have it do the job of encapsulating our core content. The title was initially wordy until our focus came into view and our "voice" took shape. Once we became even better acquainted with our subject matter, each other's writing and thinking styles, and the publisher's expectations, the title took final form. We wanted a title that was simultaneously pithy, effective in conveying the fundamental content of the book, reflective of our mutual exuberance for the topic, and something that allowed our sense of humor to peek through. It's important to be patient with this writing process, as publishers, reviewers, and readers all have an investment in what you title your work.

Why are titles so meaningful? Once something, such as an association, company, or written work, is given a title, it will have an identity. This is true even in the case of naming human beings. Parents struggle with naming their babies because grave importance is sometimes attached to a name—it signifies personal identity. Naming is embedded within deeply rooted familial and societal contexts, and it can have positive or negative associations. Titles name our acts of creation and give them reality; they are also "labels" that identify what is hopefully original, engaging work. On your vita you should see a pattern occurring among your chosen titles, suggesting that you have a focused line of inquiry. For example, regarding our own vitae, it is apparent that we share a major interest in mentoring theory and practice, faculty professional development, and graduate student learning, and that we write from clinical psychology and educational leadership perspectives.

We've heard students joke about the colon that commonly appears in published titles, of not only articles but also journals and books. This practice seems to strike them as silly and pretentious, over the top really. Academe has peculiar rituals that to the thoroughly socialized do not seem odd. To those of us who live on this side of the fence, the colon makes good sense when put to proper use: It allows for a double title, one that provides focus (the main title) and a second that allows for a more refined focus (the subtitle), as well as greater latitude for creative expression. For some writers, the use of the colon means that part of the title can be devoted to metaphoric language, interpreting creatively what the other part does descriptively. Take, for example, the journal *Taboo: The Journal of Culture and Education*, which marries the creative use of the taboo construct with the conventional academic language that follows it. In essence, the two-part title prepares readers for a radical treatment of educational content. Must colons be used in academic titles? Certainly not. This practice is optional; the writer or publisher will make the determination based on stylistic preferences and the potential for added clarity.

As you title your work, you are offering a literary "handle" for the piece and forming the scholarly identity not only of an individual publication but also of your own body of scholarship. As people read your titles, they will quickly form an impression of what you stand for and what issues you care about and want others too as well. Titles are neither arbitrary nor irrelevant. Instead, they are a kind of window into the writer's mind and soul. Keep this in the fore as you inscribe your creations.

Title your work today.

36   WORK ON ONE MANUSCRIPT AT A TIME

After all the data collection, organizing, and outlining are complete, and when you are ready to do the writing, devote yourself entirely to that manuscript. Be systematic: Shoot for linear progress—start to finish—on one project at a time. By "linear progress," we are not referring to the writing of the introduction, body, and then conclusion in any kind of pre-set or step-by-step way; rather, we refer to an ironclad commitment to completing a manuscript and getting it submitted for publication *before* moving on to the next. Although we recognize that some prolific writers are adept at a cyclical process of moving between or among several manuscripts at once, this is disorienting and probably sabotaging for most novice writers. Your undivided focus on one project at a time requires discipline, but will pay important dividends.

Writing a manuscript demands that multiple tasks be put into operation, some of which may involve new skills-building. It is likely that your writing will involve some or all of these classic skills: developing a focus and problem statement; finding a "voice" that works (first or third person); preparing an outstanding literature review; developing excellent fieldnotes, sorting and organizing data; analyzing and interpreting data, writing descriptively and with the use of concrete examples, substantiating all claims; and thoroughly editing and revising. Wolcott (2001), a famous qualitative researcher, offers these good tips in the form of an anecdotal checklist (see pp. 66–68).

The skills that go into developing a manuscript for publication review are, without a doubt, complex; as one challenge, the work will need framing in a way that situates one's particular issue within a broader picture, giving credit to those sources that have informed the idea. Along these lines, ask yourself what strategies can be used for framing the issue you are investigating and how your inquiry contributes to a particular body of literature. If you need help analyzing the data you have collected, you may need to seek support from a statistician on how to interpret your results using a particular type of software, or from a qualitative researcher on how to produce a thematic form of data analysis. Consulting handbooks in the areas in which you require assistance (e.g., data analysis and description of results) can be indispensable and substitute for on-site experts.

Different sections of your work will proceed at various stages of development and, depending on the circumstances and mood in which you find yourself, you will choose to work on specific areas. Much like building a house, while you will probably want to begin with constructing the foundation, you will have a great deal of latitude as to how you develop the project, but consider estimating times to completion for each task.

For the manuscript writing, throw yourself in and, until you get to the editing-and-revising stage, throw your perfectionism out the window. Replace anal-retentive and obsessive-compulsive tendencies with tolerance for "shitty first drafts" (SFD), which according to novelist Lamott (1994) are much like "the child's draft, where you let it all pour out and then let it romp all over the place, knowing that no one is going to see it and that you can shape it later" (pp. 21–22). The SFD, if you will, is the writer's "channel" for "whatever voices and visions come through and onto the page" (p. 23). Although Lamott's context is not academe, novice writers should find it reassuring that even accomplished writers lack verbal precision and free-flowing self-confidence when approaching the writing task; very few writers produce eloquent first drafts. Lamott further attests that most writers learn what they are doing *during* the act of writing itself, not at the outset. Arriving at a polished product demands a willingness to first wade into the muck and produce words—even when the way is unclear.

Nonetheless, most new, and probably experienced professors as well, function best when they have a sense of direction, and so it is advisable to prepare flexible blueprints in the form of outlines and proposals. These will serve as a preliminary synopsis of your topic, focus, research question(s), setting, methods, key participants, and references—anything that's relevant. Proposals may change as you go about investigating your subject. Novice writers end up with a more focused and coherent study when they plan, brainstorm, and problem-solve with their peers and with experts, and in ways consistent with the research paradigm in their specific disciplines.

Expect to have downtime when you are working on a single project. Delay can happen when writing with authors who are busy working on your parts or doing their own, and especially when your writing is being reviewed or is in production. But do not allow for delay to obstruct your writing progress. Strategic planning is essential to keeping the pen (and mind) moving. As Wolcott (2001) advises, work on one project at a time but also turn to another project when your writing is temporarily blocked due to a tardy colleague, time-consuming data collection or analysis, or editorial review. Don't get caught short with nothing to write during any waiting periods! We naturally seek alternatives in our lives when the unexpected happens. Take the simple example of dining out: When a restaurant that you've arrived at is closed, you turn around and find another that is open. Failing to do so will leave you frustrated (and hungry). Follow this metaphor in your writing life: When work is necessarily suspended on your current project, always have several others waiting in the cue.

In time, you may find yourself able to work on multiple projects simultaneously without sacrificing the attention you give to teaching and life. But for now keep one foot in front of the other. And keep an extra pair of sneakers ready and a research map handy should you unexpectedly have to take a different direction.

37   GENERATE MULTIPLE PRODUCTS WHEN POSSIBLE

Write smart: Efficient writers have a knack for conceptualizing writing projects in "clusters." Rather than writing a single article on a topic and moving on, the prolific scholar conceptualizes a program or string of publications on a topic; each discrete article leads to a follow-up extension, an application to a different subject group, or a summative review and theoretical piece. Spin-offs, extensions, and serial investigations in a single area can markedly economize writing time while adding to the volume of your accomplishments.

Experienced writers are good at getting the "biggest bang for their buck" when it comes to preparing the same work for multiple outcomes, usually grant funding, presentation, and publication. Outstanding scholars sometimes prepare the same paper not only for refereed publication but also for nonrefereed (sometimes invited) publication; these shorter, more accessible pieces appear in high-distribution presses, such as association-sponsored newsletters and newspapers. Similarly, a juried presentation is turned into a local presentation sponsored by the university or community. Take, for example, the grant application that Carol put together on what aspiring school leaders most need to know about the role of site-based leadership and what faculty who teach in principal preparation programs need to know in the way of relevant curriculum. The funded grant turned into a journal article that was published in a national-level journal, a book that was published with a leading publisher, and two presentations, one of national stature and the other a local conference. The short and long works were crafted with entirely different but related foci, as were the two presentations.

Beyond submitting your work for both publication and presentation, smart writing involves strategizing early on how to create multiple manuscripts in a focused area. For example,

Brad became interested in the issue of screening professional psychologists for moral character and psychological fitness. Even before an initial theoretical article on the issue was completed, a second project involving a survey of training directors on the topic was underway. Shortly thereafter, a review of state licensing guidelines bearing on character and fitness was completed. As of this writing, a fourth article offering proposed screening templates is under review. Quite often, a good idea has multiple implications and applications. An innovative theory or research question lends itself to empirical pieces, theoretical manuscripts, applied or practice articles, and summative literature reviews.

It is a legitimate scholarly practice to publish and present different facets of your work in different venues—especially when the original data or idea is large or complex. But seek counsel as you go, in order to avoid duplication and any ethical snags. Novice writers often ask whether they can use the same data set (e.g., survey responses, interview transcriptions) for two different articles. We understand that this is, generally speaking, an acceptable practice, just as long as the write up itself is different and just as long as an acknowledgment of the overlap appears in the manuscript and in the letter prepared for the editor. However, not all editors, publishers, administrators, or even scholars are comfortable with this practice, believing that once data have been published they should *not* appear in another published form. In crude terms, they might label this behavior "double dipping." So be aware, find out what's permissible in your field, and above all, be transparent with editors and publishers when submitting multiple manuscripts based on a single data source.

Although it is imperative to avoid duplicating or plagiarizing your own work, many well-known scholars have, in fact, built their entire careers around a single data set. As one colleague in the arts and sciences has pointed out, the use of Shakespeare's plays as "data" for ongoing writing is considered a legitimate practice in her discipline, just as it would be for any other literary body of work. As another example, we know leading scholars who have used in their various articles the same multi-year data from a single school project. In some cases, a gargantuan data set can keep a researcher busy for years with myriad publications—each legitimately unique in scope and focus. Here's the bottom line: It is a legitimate scholarly practice to generate multiple products from a single theoretical innovation or empirical data set, but avoid outright duplication of your work and always apprise editors of any overlap in your manuscripts. Finally, stay in tune with normative practice in your discipline and stay abreast of your comfort level and insights gained from consultations with productive scholars and decision-makers.

38   WRITE PROGRAMMATICALLY—MAINTAIN A FOCUS

Once you know what you love to research or write about, consider making this your niche—at least for the time it takes you to get promoted and tenured. Think of your niche as a program of sequential publications within a focused area of your discipline. Write pieces that are integral to your scholarly agenda and that are related in some way, typically thematically, philosophically, or even methodologically. Professors have built entire individual scholarly programs around such specific niches as themes in the novels of Walker Percy, computerized economic prediction models for Peru, cross-race or -gender mentoring dynamics in organizations, and the efficacy of varied reinforcement schedules on the behavior of rats. One of us once had a colleague whose entire scholarly focus was on the metabolism of hummingbirds! You get the idea. A niche is a highly defined area of scholarly focus. The more specific the niche, the more quickly you are likely to become an identified expert on the topic.

Although some prolific scholars are perpetual leap toads—jumping from topic to topic as their interests or opportunities change—this approach seldom pays for new academics. Figure out the pattern you want to create early on and then, as needed, improvise. Tenure and promotion committees are particularly interested in a scholar's "line of inquiry" or "stream" of publications supported by a coherent and overarching topic of study. In most cases, a solid scholarly niche will help establish your expertise, generate greater attention from other scholars in the area, and often lead to invitations to contribute to multi-authored volumes or collaborative projects. Although the idea of picking a topic to stick with for years may sound daunting, do not despair. Once you establish a strong record of accomplishment— often sometime after successfully clearing the promotion and tenure hurdle—you will have earned the right to write about anything you want. At that time, you can move freely among topics as your interests change.

Writing programmatically is a supreme artistic and emotional, intellectual, and mental challenge. Even at its most fundamental and routine, the development of a focused area of study takes imagination, not just toil. This helps to explain why some accomplished writers who have well-developed scholarly programs find that they must complete one significant piece before shifting. Otherwise, they will become overwhelmed and lose their focus. One such tenured professor's scholarly program, situated within educational technology and media studies, has three foci: the visualization of multivariate data; learning from static graphic displays; and the cognitive capacities of new media. He shared with us that, because he can only take "one analytical bite at a time," he would not want to simultaneously tackle more than one project. The types of experiments he conducts involve multiple variables and complicated analyses, making it necessary for him to hold in his mind numerous interacting variables in order to make sense of the problem being studied. This mental process, he explained, taxes to the fullest his creative capacity and attention to detail. Metaphorically, this researcher attends to one "canvas" at a time, but his experience of any "single canvas" is nonlinear; further, each work is nestled within, not apart from, his scholarly program.

This leads us to ask, what is the focus of your scholarly program and what are its key elements and defining features? How do you draw the contours between your niche and the larger scholarly discipline? What steps have you taken to articulate your agenda on paper and to share it with others? Making this effort at the time of and for the purpose of tenure review is simply too late; it is no easy task to define the pattern underlying one's work and the relationships among all of the major parts (e.g., ideas, commitments) and products (e.g., articles, chapters).

Consider studying the scholarly program of accomplished academics: Learn how they have conceptualized what they are about and how they make sense of old and new projects within the context of the whole. Great scholars have a knack for inventing their own future by imagining or intuiting what they want to accomplish before taking action (Hoyle, 1995). They see the big picture, much like an original musical composer who "hears" a symphony in its entirety, including the resonating parts of the cello, piano, violin, and other instruments. In order to get a glimpse of how a successful scholarly niche might unfold in your own field of scholarship, access the primary literature search engine in your discipline and search for the publications of two or three of the topic scholars you refer to in your own work. By scrolling through their publications over the decades, you will develop an appreciation for programmatic writing in a focused area. You will probably note that they are often contributors to themed volumes or journals bearing on their area of expertise. And while there may be occasional cul-de-sacs and dead ends in their writing, their ability to maintain consistency in focus over many years offers one key to success as an academic writer.

Here is an academic scoop: The more specific your area of expertise and the more productive you are within your specialty area, the more rapidly you will be identified as a rising star from the broader scholarly world and the more frequently you will be invited to contribute to special issues of journals, edited volumes, and book projects. Simultaneously, you will be sought after as an editor, contributor, speaker, program organizer, symposia participant, grants writer, and more in your area. Call this the *snowball effect* of programmatic or niche-based scholarship: The more clearly and actively you define a personal research focus and then write consistently within it, the more rapidly outside opportunities for greater productivity will come beckoning.

Invent your own future today. Develop a program of study that defines who you are as a scholar and relate all you do to it.

39   PICK THE LOW-HANGING FRUIT FIRST

Get the easiest stuff done first. For new faculty, there are many publications just waiting to be written or simply finalized before larger, more time-consuming, or longitudinal things get tackled. These easier items might include pieces based on a dissertation, collaboration with a graduate school mentor, or even collaboration with faculty in your new department who invite you to contribute something worthwhile to projects almost ready for publication review. There are also shorter pieces for less competitive peer-reviewed journals that could be quickly written and submitted. By doing this, the new professor gets some products in the cue and some publication entries stacked up on the vita. If these are neglected, it might be a mistake, in that bigger, more challenging, and lower probability projects carry greater risk of little return (at least at first) on the investment. And, as we know, new faculty need pubs and more pubs!

Here's a strategic, thought-provoking question for any new professor to seriously consider: What projects could you most reasonably bring to completion quickly? Very often, you can carve your dissertation into several distinct journal articles or prepare it as a book. This rich source of scholarship is just waiting to be mined. Partial manuscripts may stand ready for rapid completion and unanalyzed data sets may be ready for analysis: Devote the modest time required to bring these easily accessible products to fruition. Getting a string of publications in motion can be jumpstarted by beginning with the projects that are closest to completion at the start. We call this picking the low-hanging fruit. It is an ideal way to generate momentum in your writing career. Once your scholarship is in motion, its inertia will often pull you along.

Another way of addressing "low-hanging fruit" is to give priority to major projects for which others or yourself have been contracted—most often edited volumes. But check first with decision makers in your department or college to see if these products are accorded adequate credit in your institution's tenure-and-promotion accounting system. Because refereed journal articles are so heavily weighed, books in the social sciences, including education, are usually only encouraged after tenure has been awarded, whereas in the humanities books are everything at every stage of the review process. However, peer-reviewed book chapters also count as weighted publications, so think about contributing to others' larger works where you feel relatively certain these projects will see the light of day in volumes by respected publishers.

In the right circumstances, then, edited volumes are premium examples of low-hanging fruit. If you decide to go ahead and write a chapter for someone's book, be sure that the work has been contracted before proceeding. Keep in mind that a signed contract is no guarantee that the book's editor will succeed at meeting his or her obligations. Editors and publishers can stall the project for so long that it doesn't come to fruition, and companies can go out of business, especially new and obscure publishing houses. However, contracts normally carry the guarantee of publication as long as the author meets the agreed-upon publishing terms: These typically feature the completion date of the manuscript, the timeliness of any revisions, and the production of a high-quality work, including any required sections and components (e.g., appendices, glossaries, and indexes).

Books and monographs come in many forms, including single-authored and coauthored works, edited volumes, and collections of various kinds. If you want to write a book that is not based on your dissertation, consider doing it with reliable and talented colleagues who have already published books with excellent publishers. You can also join an existing editorial team and co-produce a book that features the contributions of leading scholars (or at least competent writers) in your field. One of us wrote a book that relied solely on graduate students as contributors, a project that took an inordinate amount of time due to the mentoring that had to occur regarding sound scholarship and the extensive hands-on rewriting that became necessary in order to get the chapters into good shape. However, the author was tenured at the time, so this all-out effort did not create a problem. Clearly, working with novice writers, whether on books or articles, might not be a good idea for most tenure-earning faculty.

Keep in mind that books don't need to be written from beginning to end by single authors; they come in myriad forms. While tenure-earning, one of us did pick the low-hanging fruit on our own writing tree by turning the dissertation into a single-authored book but then three more books materialized during the five-year timeframe—these were coauthored with dynamic teams of professors, students, and teachers. We nurtured our own fruit tree, so to speak, by picking the fruit from the bottom to the top. Imagine your publication world as a fruit tree—what "low-hanging fruit" might be within reach and how far do you need to climb to get it? What projects could be brought to completion within reasonably short fixed periods and which are better left to the post-tenure climb?

Before taking on prolonged writing projects higher up "the tree," be smart—generate momentum and sustenance for the journey with low-hanging fruit first.

40   OVERESTIMATE TIME TO COMPLETION

When estimating how long it will take to complete a scholarly work, such as a book chapter, book, or monograph, be conservative. In most cases, major writing projects take (much) longer than anticipated. Famed psychologist/author Harriet Rheingold (1994) recommended multiplying your initial time estimate by a factor of four. Generally, you will want to overestimate the time to completion. When working with editors and publishers, it is important to create a reputation for punctuality and dependability. One way of doing this is to produce timely manuscript reviews for editors seeking volunteers. It is always better to turn your reviews or manuscripts in early than late.

Always overestimate the time it will require you to write an article, book chapter, or book. Why? First, as noted previously, editors and publishers simply fall in love with dependable writers. Sadly, punctual delivery of contracted or agreed upon writing products can be so rare in academe that a writer who proves that he or she delivers consistently on or before deadlines will certainly be in high demand and, consequently, will enjoy far more future "green lights" from publishers. Second, overestimating the time to completion builds in plenty of discretionary time for changing your work, pursuing time-consuming side trails—if you have a penchant for doing so, and generally enjoying the process more. You will also be better prepared to stop working and tend to the exigencies of life and family when these impinge. Third, being generous when estimating deadlines and delivery dates will help you avoid the angst that goes with falling behind. We both have several colleagues who are chronically behind—constantly juggling a significant number of projects and growing increasingly anxious. Cognitive psychologists would say their lives are filled with Zeigarnicks. The *Zeigarnick effect* is a well-established principle that holds that people remember uncompleted or interrupted tasks better than completed ones. When an academic has too many Zeigarnicks hanging around, life can become one steady stream of worry and fret about getting things wrapped up.

We all need intention and focus, as well as purpose and motivation if we expect to succeed in the academy. By combining a sense of purpose with your intention to succeed, you will be more mindful of critical tasks and goals—deadlines will fall more naturally into place. A "fire in the belly," when blended with effective organization and scheduling, is a driver for getting work done in a timely manner. In addition, prolific writers are known for having a well-functioning prospective memory; they are diligent when it comes to future tasks and associated deadlines. Remind yourself of important deadlines by maintaining such up-to-date memory joggers as daily, weekly, and monthly lists, but more importantly, make sure deadlines are reasonable before you agree to them. Consult editors, fellow writers, particular reference books, or anything else that will help clarify this for you.

Two mechanisms may be at work for those writers who are perpetually late in meeting deadlines: avoidance of starting (and completing) a task, and perfectionism. Now, by perfectionism we are not referring to the high-quality standards that must be met in order to satisfy one's goals. Leading scholars, like Olympic athletes or celebrity artists, would probably scoff at the idea that the work they make public can afford to be anything less than "perfect"—that is, short of the ideal. All scholars should pursue excellence, but there is sometimes a fine line between excellence and perfectionism.

Perfectionism is generally rooted in irrational beliefs—most often demands for superhuman performance. Perfectionistic demands inhibit productivity. Because the author fears not doing well enough, he or she falls prey to the irrational belief that perfection must be achieved if our work is to have meaning (Messina & Messina, 2006). Some "perfectionists" are out of touch with their proclivity to be perfect. Here's a case in point: A tenure-earning female we spoke with might qualify as an "archetypal" perfectionist in that she works well ahead of time and manically on scholarly tasks that must be completed within a specified timeframe right up to the last minute, including proposals for grants and conferences. She has compensated for this obsessive behavior by learning how to push the envelope on a deadline, knowing all about the dreaded consequence of electronic lockout at the Internet websites of professional associations. She has playfully nicknamed this automated mechanism of proposal-blocking the "brick wall." After the "wall" comes up on proposal submissions, this professor then goes "on the hunt," pursuing individuals in charge who might empathize and let her submit late; she says that her charm is her greatest resource at such times. Her lifelong problematic behavior persists because, as she revealed, she always underestimates not only the time for actual completion of critical tasks, even though the work she does is of exceptional quality, but also her own ability to get the work done. Panic sets in at the last minute; perfectionism, fueled by self-doubt, is really a manifestation of deep-seated insecurity for this academic Psychoanalysis aside, it is of deep concern that a faculty member would constantly set up roadblocks to her own well-being.

Another self-proclaimed perfectionist explained that he loses sight of how long it should take to complete a task once his perfectionism kicks in. He cited the example of a creative drawing that he decided to include, at the last minute, in a grant application, commenting, "Although the figure didn't *have* to be in there at all, let alone as a work of art, it nevertheless reached that standard." On a positive note, he has been gradually remedying his ways through better and more conscious planning. He used the metaphor of an airport terminal to capture the significant change in his life habits: Before, he was always arriving late only to experience the frustration of the doors closing in front of him; while he is still running to catch the plane, doors are now closing behind him. He doesn't expect that he will ever be the kind of person who has planned his arrival time with such accuracy that there is time to relax in the terminal.

If you struggle with perfectionism, or if you are easily derailed or distracted by enticing side-roads en route to project completion, then by all means, either build time for such delays into your scheduling estimates or—better yet—find a way to knock off the perfectionism and distraction!

As discussed elsewhere in this text, time management skills also influence the ability to complete tasks in a timely manner. However, not all efforts need be handled well in advance, certainly not when it comes to service anyway. Prioritize your academic writing; do your own scholarly writing each day and week before attending to service activities (e.g., search committee reports). We suggest that you complete any such service-related work within a compressed time so that you do not lapse into being more thorough (or perfectionistic) than is necessary. If you are entering a period of demanding service, liberally factor this into your project timelines. Tips for toning down perfectionism include avoid rewriting a proposal multiple times, resist searching for the exact, perfect quote to use in something you are writing, and establishing a clear cut-off point for completing a work or submitting a proposal or project for review.

41   It's All about Quality (and Quantity Matters too)

Deans, department chairs, and promotion committees are all fond of insisting that the quality of faculty publications is what matters most. While the quality of journals and presses is certainly a salient factor when assessing a scholar's contribution to the field or preparedness for promotion and tenure, the fact remains that sheer volume of published material also carries weight—it is difficult to ignore a heavy vita! Commit to generating a steady stream of publications and developing a curriculum vita that reveals a healthy pattern over time. This takes time, of course. As long as the journals you select are reputable, it is preferential to generate a solid list of peer-reviewed work instead of gambling that your peers will regard your sparse publications as monumental contributions to the field, and thus worthy of tenure or promotion. When in doubt, seek advice about local tenure-and-promotion norms from your department chair or institutional mentor.

Although rare indeed, a single published work in a top-tier outlet or a piece with profound impact on the field can make a bigger impact on your station in academe than 50 mediocre works in low-level journals. One of us knows an academic whose published dissertation made her famous in her discipline—from the United States she moved to a European institution where she was academically advanced without any additional publications. As another twist on the norm, renegade scholars and paradigm busters in the academy have sometimes been forced to turn to low-quality journals or renowned ones outside their field—the leading presses within their own discipline would not publish what seemed outlandish at the time. Later on, their peers finally acknowledged their groundbreaking work as seminal, even extraordinary. Take, for example, British psychologist Sir Frederic Bartlett, whose schema construct was not compatible with the worldview that was dominant in psychology during the 1930s and for some time after that; hence, his original thinking was not accepted by mainstream memory researchers. Bartlett's work is the intellectual precursor to the schema construct in cognitive science, through such renowned individuals as the philosopher Immanuel Kant and the developmental psychologist Jean Piaget.

But be warned: Cinderella stories are outliers in the academy. It is improbable that you will publish a single defining study—instead, count on the timeless correlation between the solid production of high-quality works and recognition or impact. Publish with regularity and with peer-reviewed presses—this is the assurance we as scholars offer that quality standards are being upheld and that expectations for productivity are being satisfied. Positive assessment by one's peers who review our scholarly work using high standards set by editors and publishers is what communicates quality in our profession. It is always preferable to publish even a modest number of works appearing in excellent journals. The publication of a hundred articles in low-tier journals, especially those with high acceptance rates or flimsy online venues, will only serve to cast doubt on the rigor and impact of your work.

Don't wait for that one home run—recognition, when it does come, tends to happen gradually. Quite often, those striving to make a difference will likely not know the extent to which their efforts are having an impact. Citation by others is a major signal that others are recognizing your work, as is the granting of major honors and awards.

Be your own best sponsor: Promote your quality work for award consideration, especially at the national level but also the state and local levels. As one example, many leading associations now provide early career awards to new faculty. Years ago one of us submitted our second book (a coedited volume) for award consideration to a premier association in education and received the honor for outstanding research. This catapulted the text into its second edition, additional awards, and invitations to speak. If permissible, nominate your own relevant publications; however, for major awards a nominator must do this, so find someone with an established reputation in the field to sponsor you. Awards affirm to the world the quality and merit of your work. While recognition and acknowledgment of different kinds, such as unprompted correspondence from others (e.g., faculty, students) and invited talks can also approximate this, significant awards occupy a revered status all their own.

Here's a good tip: Investigate and keep track of the acceptance/rejection rates of your journals. Practice quality control oversight. Typically, in order to establish the quality of the journals you have published in for the purpose of tenure and promotion, a thorough list of journals and their rejection rates is required. It is especially important for you to provide this data for tenure-and-promotion or award committees at smaller institutions, or even in larger institutions when the committee is composed of scholars from other disciplines. You may also list subscription and circulation rates, which can be secondary markers of quality. Identify the rates of acceptance either by asking the relevant editors and publishers directly or by consulting an official guide, notably *Cabell's Dictionary* or the Web of Science.

Finally, quality without quantity, and certainly quantity without quality, are not strategies that will enable most of us to achieve academic success. Your dean and department chair are right: Quality does matter, but volume helps. Strive for balance.

7

REVISE, EDIT, AND REVISE
SOME MORE

Editors and publishers do not tolerate mediocrity in author's works, so edit yourself thoroughly. Learn the art of mindfully and thoroughly revising your own work by practicing the strategies we share in this chapter. Practice parsimony: Whether at the level of words, ideas, assumptions, or source citations, express key points in the most parsimonious language. Edit yourself so carefully that your writing is spare and crystal clear without sacrificing thoroughness and completeness. Return revisions immediately: We offer established procedural guidelines for responding to an editor's request for revision of your work.

42   MEDIOCRITY IS *NOT* ALLOWED—EDIT YOURSELF THOROUGHLY

As a scholar on a mission to rack up many solid publications, you do not have time to waste having manuscripts rejected outright or held up in an elongated editorial review process simply because of lousy technical preparation and proofreading. Our experience as writers and editors has taught that in the business of writing, nothing dooms a professor to obscurity and failure more quickly than mediocre preparation of manuscripts.

Think, for a moment, from the perspective of a journal editor, an authority in your area of interest, who screens the quality of works received. Your job is hectic! You are responsible for publishing high-quality issues throughout the year; inundated with manuscripts, you want to save your best reviewers for those manuscripts that show strong promise of eventually being accepted—the rest will need to be rejected outright. The very last thing you have time or patience for is lousy writing or manuscripts filled with unnecessary grammatical errors—reviewers express surprise at seeing sloppy and erroneous material submitted for publication review. As a steady stream of unremarkable manuscripts flows across your desk, along comes a clean, pithy, beautifully written, and carefully prepared manuscript.

You sit up and take notice.

Upon further inspection you notice there are no apparent spelling or grammatical errors, the references are scrupulously in compliance with the journal's required style, and the author has obviously read and followed the publication's specific requirements—including manuscript length, table and figure preparation, and even the contents of the cover letter.

You are intrigued. Consciously or unconsciously, your regard for the author has solidified and it is positive indeed.

This is how it works. By nurturing personal intolerance for mediocrity in your own work, you quickly gain the respect of editors and their boards and significantly increase the probability of getting not only the current manuscript accepted, but subsequent manuscripts as well. Excellent attention to detail—when coupled with solid scholarship—creates a positive halo in the minds of editors and reviewers alike. Your reputation will develop positive inertia such that when an editor receives a new manuscript from you, he or she will assume top-notch work until proven otherwise. And this is the reception we all want our work to receive.

If there is one thing you must understand about scholarly writing, it is this: *When the writing is done, your work is not.* This is a terribly hard lesson for many of us. Often, the work of crafting an article or a book chapter is so arduous that writing the summary and adding the final references feels like the end of the line. With the final keystroke, we are all too ready to drop the thing in the mail or hit the electronic "submit" button—eager to experience the satisfaction and emotional catharsis that goes with completion. But to succeed at publishing, you must resist the siren call of premature submission and accept the fact that finishing the first draft is only the initial step; editing your work thoroughly and repeatedly before submitting it is essential, as is the effort inherent in revising your work according to editorial and reviewer comments following the initial review.

Once you have finished your first draft of any piece of scholarly work, we recommend that you print it, put it away, and go on to something else. Return to your new manuscript refreshed and determined to critically edit. After reading through your work, mark it liberally with pen on hard copy or with "track changes" on electronic copy. Work on the sentence structure and word usage; be especially careful to avoid redundancy in vocabulary, and be vigilant to the laws of grammar. If you struggle with grammar, obtain a copy of *The Elements of Style* (Strunk & White, 2000) and learn its contents inside and out. Be careful to ensure that your introduction and rationale for the article jibe with the actual contents; likewise, be certain that you have not introduced important concepts in the summary or conclusions without first addressing them in the heart of your work. Review each reference carefully and be sure citations in the text match those in the bibliography.

Some authors prefer to attend to all of these important editorial concerns simultaneously as they reread. Others would rather read the full manuscript more than once, each time attending to a different element (e.g., grammar, spelling, word usage, references). Whatever your preference, we encourage you to improve upon and correct your manuscript by thoroughly going through it several times, each time making the changes and reprinting the entire thing before starting over. Your goal is to catch all of the grammatical and stylistic problems yourself and to slowly hone the writing such that it becomes precise and pithy.

After you are convinced that further reading on your part will be unlikely to yield additional corrections, it is time to approach at least one trusted colleague—someone who also happens to be an excellent writer or editor—and ask him or her to critique your work before submitting it. Of course, you must avoid imposing on colleagues. This is why developing a mutually beneficial critiquing partnership is wise. After you have received at least one external critique, make recommended changes, do your own final read through and then double check the intended outlet's publication guidelines for specific stylistic requirements. Be certain that your work is in full compliance. You may also wish to solicit, on your final version, the helpful input of a professional copyeditor or proofreader, who will catch problems and errors and strengthen the overall work.

Now, it is time to submit your work. We close this chapter with some advice about combating mediocrity. We have already suggested that nothing will sabotage your chances of getting work into print faster than sloppy manuscript preparation. If you are someone who struggles mightily with the willpower required to bear down and edit carefully after the writing is done, then for your own sake, honestly evaluate the source of your resistance and address it. Common reasons for submitting mediocre manuscripts (beyond poor scholarship) include

1. impatience—"I'm so excited to get this off to the publisher, I just can't wait;"
2. low frustration tolerance—"I can't stand the tedium involved in proofreading and editing my work repeatedly;"
3. narcissism—"I am a scholar not an editor; I can't be troubled with the minutia!" or
4. an inability to read one's own work critically and to apply the conventions of proper grammar and formatting: "I never had the chance to learn writing-and-formatting norms at any point in my education, so I can't be blamed for what I haven't been taught."

If any of these sound familiar, we have news for you: You absolutely can stand to edit and are expected to, and your attention to minutia will matter a great deal to most editors and reviewers.

Decide early on that writing a good piece of scholarship always involves setting aside time for thoroughgoing editing. Avoid submitting your work prematurely. Strive to create and submit flawlessly prepared manuscripts that reflect well on you.

43   IN WORDS, PRACTICE PARSIMONY

One of the most vexing problems for new writers is the predilection toward wordy prose. Editors the world over tell us that in writing, less is more. When engaged in typing words into a document, practice extreme economy. The parsimonious writer is frugal, stingy, and austere when it comes to allowing words admission to the printed page. In a word, seek *simplicity* in your written expression.

Because the temptation to add unnecessary words is so powerful, it is doubly important to revise your own work mercilessly; you must be willing to slash superfluous words, eliminate redundancy, and forego side points, all to ensure clarity. When proofreading, be skeptical regarding the necessity or value of each word, sentence, paragraph, and section. We recommend learning about economy of word usage by reading authors such as William Shakespeare, Evelyn Waugh, Earnest Hemingway, J. B. S. Haldane, or D'Arcy Thompson.

Practice tapestry approaches to writing by organizing words, ideas, and sections into coherent patterns. When reviewing and editing manuscripts, we notice that many new authors get bogged down in lengthy reviews of the existing literature—often describing relevant studies one-by-one instead of weaving the previous literature together into coherent categories or themes. Remember, not every published study or article in your area of focus merits mention; set criteria for inclusion of material in your literature review, clarify the criteria for readers, and then abide by them. And studies that do merit mention may be easily clustered in brief paragraphs or even sentences—each does not require a separate critical review. On the other hand, be sure that your sources are current; when possible, reference some publications from the current year. Parsimony does not mean leaving out critical information: Editors find that papers not including sources within the last few years tend to be viewed unfavorably by reviewers unless an explanation is provided within the work itself.

In the sciences, the principle of parsimony—sometimes called *Occam's razor*—advocates avoiding unnecessary assumptions. There is a longstanding tradition in science that simpler models are more likely to be correct than complex ones. It seems that nature—like journal and book editors—prefers simplicity. Whether choosing theoretical models or explaining them in prose, always select the simplest option.

If you repeat yourself in a manuscript, if you belabor the main point, or if you suffer from wordy prose, you are likely to lose readers and frustrate reviewers. Many editors we know are fond of saying "tighten up the writing" in feedback to authors. Here is the translation of this criticism: Slash unnecessary words, express key points in the most parsimonious language, and edit yourself so carefully that your writing is spare and crystal clear.

44   RETURN REVISIONS IMMEDIATELY

You have written with parsimony, assiduously edited your work, and finally, the manuscript is off to the journal editor. You have high hopes as you list the manuscript on your vita as "in review." Then, because the typical review period ranges widely, anywhere from two to five or even seven months, you go about the business of teaching, service, and working on other scholarly projects. When least expected, a letter from the editor appears in your mailbox or e-mail account; with senses suddenly heightened, you open it. In our rich fantasy worlds, editor's letters always read something like this:

> Dear Dr. _____,
>
> Let me thank you for writing one of the finest pieces of scholarship I have ever laid eyes on. It is perfect. As a matter of fact, I learned a lot about your area of expertise, and even more about the art of writing just from reading it. All my reviewers loved it too and begged me to ask you not to change a thing. Not only am I accepting your work without revision, but I would also like to formally accept your next manuscript right now. Your work is so important; I am waiving it to the front of the journal's list of accepted manuscripts to speed publication. Let me thank you again for submitting this gem. I have enclosed the original copy and if you would indulge me, I'm hoping you'll autograph it for me and allow me to formally nominate it for a national award.
>
> The Editor

Sadly, it is about then that we wake up and read the actual letter. In our experience, it is profoundly rare to have a manuscript of any kind accepted outright. Although this does happen on occasion, it may say more about the quality or needs of the journal or the expertise of the review board than it does about your work. Quality peer reviewers and experienced editors can nearly always help a scholar improve both the content and quality of a manuscript before it is formally accepted. In most cases, assuming that your original manuscript is not rejected outright, the editor will either reject the work but invite a resubmission following substantial revision, or will accept the manuscript pending significant changes.

Here is the good news: When an editor does not outright reject a piece, there is high probability that it will eventually be published if you move on the revision quickly and respond thoroughly to the requested changes. Think of the editor's letter as merely one more step in the curious dance of publication between writer and editor that begins when you first submit your work. Having received the initial editorial response, and assuming your partner, the editor, has not exited the dance floor with a flat-out rejection, it is now your turn to muster some courage and show your best moves as you prepare an impressive revision.

One of the simplest ways to ensure that good projects and potential publications die on the vine is to drag your feet on generating a revised manuscript. When word from the editor is anything but a firm rejection, you must adopt a "can-do" mindset and force yourself to get the revision done quickly and thoroughly. To do anything else is to sabotage your success as a writer. Revising work—sometimes repeatedly—is one of the mainstay activities of the most prolific scholars. There are a number of reasons why unsuccessful academics fail to revise and resubmit their work: Some may do poorly when it comes to responding adaptively to disappointment. Some scholars become overly ego-involved in their manuscripts and have trouble accepting constructive criticism of their work; comments from reviewers and revision requests from editors are erroneously perceived as injurious attacks on the author or his or her ideology, values, methods, or something else—in this case, anger may undermine an effective response. Still others are prone to shame and self-doubt that hamper the confidence needed to assume the best-case scenario that leads to successful revision of one's work.

In order to respond effectively to an editor's request for revision of your work, we offer the following procedural guidelines. These steps not only provide a clear framework for walking through an effective response, they have worked well for a multitude of prolific academic writers—many of whom will tell you that responding effectively and expeditiously to publishers is nonnegotiable, and moreover, the key to productivity.

1. When you receive the editor's letter read it slowly and carefully, as well as all the enclosed reviews.
2. Put the letter and the reviews away for a while. This may mean several hours or a week—depending on the author. This time-out period allows space for the most salient comments to sink in, for possible approaches to the revision to percolate, and for decision making to occur.
3. When you have worked through your initial deflation and possible injuries to your ego, as well as any feelings of anger and depression, pull out the file containing your manuscript, along with the editorial materials. Read your manuscript (it will have been several days, weeks, or months) and then read each review again. What at first registered as caustic comments and impossible revision requests may now begin to feel like constructive criticisms and revision ideas that make good sense.
4. Use a highlighter to emphasize the editor and reviewers' key points and recommendations—quite often these will overlap.
5. Prioritize your revisions. And always start with the recommendations and requests made by the editor. In our experience, the editor's letter will distill those reviewer comments and recommendations that the editor deems most valid and vital to a solid revision. Ignoring an editor's request is generally a bad idea.
6. After addressing the editor's concerns, attend to those reviewer comments not covered by the editor's letter but that nonetheless appear valid and reasonable. In many cases, reviewers are invested in improving the quality of manuscripts published by the journal. No matter their tone, think of them as consultants, not critics.

7. In many cases, it is not imperative that you address every reviewer criticism. Some will be idiosyncratic or superfluous—perhaps reflecting the reviewer's pet peeves, theoretical biases, or down-right misunderstandings. But try to be objective and consider each recommendation carefully.

8. Keep careful track of all of the revisions you make, along with the relevant pages in the revised manuscripts where each change can be located.

9. After each and every revision is complete, craft a detailed cover letter addressed to the editor that spells out your approach to the modification or change. Be sure to briefly outline each change you made and how each one addresses the editorial and reviewer feedback. You may wish to include the actual changes, verbatim, in your letter or just paraphrase them depending upon what works best. Leave no room for speculation about whether you took into account each concern. For any instances in which you may have elected not to make a recommended change, offer a clear, cordial, and convincing rationale.

10. In the cover letter, be sure to express both gratitude for the excellent feedback and appreciation for the opportunity to revise and resubmit your work. Also, clarify your willingness to make additional modifications as needed.

11. Do a final read through and edit of your manuscript. Because many changes have been made, you must approach the editing task anew—as though this is the first draft of your work. Attend to the minutia!

12. On your revised work, solicit feedback from a capable, trusted colleague and, if necessary, a good copyeditor or proofreader.

In most cases, this editorial writing procedure—when expeditious and thorough—will significantly increase the probability that your good manuscript will be improved and that your improved manuscript will be accepted for publication.

8

SEEK MENTORS, MENTORING
NETWORKS, AND
WRITING COACHES

This section focuses on helpful ideas and strategies for getting you the support you need to become a productive scholar. It is important that you try to maximize productive mentoring relationships by drawing from past and current relationships; notably, you can make good use of both formal and informal mentoring relationships to the benefit of your work. Seek one or more writing mentors, but be selective; you will want to establish relationships with productive academics who are responsive and who have time. Mentors and coaches may be found inside and outside of your immediate unit or university. Also, access writing coaches for specific writing-related concerns and for brief periods. No matter your experience at other institutions, use faculty mentors to learn local academic cultural norms. Prolific faculty will understand the cultural context in which you are employed and the unique "personality" of your institution. Ask questions and turn to seasoned guides to master the norms governing the local writing milieu. Avail yourself of the benefits of good mentoring, networking, and coaching and reflect on why you may not be doing so should this be the case.

45 MAXIMIZE PRODUCTIVE
MENTORING RELATIONSHIPS

Here's a good scholarly strategy: Stick with graduate school mentorships or other useful relationships that have helped to facilitate your productivity in the past. Also give serious consideration to seeking new mentors—either by tapping into "formal" matching systems in the institution for new faculty or by going out on your own and targeting really prolific and helpful senior colleagues. Additionally, mentors can be found through personal contacts as well as professional organizations, listserves, electronic chatrooms, and more. Virtual mentors who work online with rising scholars have been known to contribute a great deal to their progress and success.

Remember that you stand to benefit from both formal and informal mentoring. Formal mentoring occurs between individuals or within groups/cohorts whereby the conditions have been established for mentoring and whereby the institution recognizes the work. Examples include new faculty mentoring programs sponsored by departments, colleges, and universities, as well as state and national professional associations. Take advantage of sessions on writing for scholarly publication, mentoring roundtables focused on journal publication, and special interest groups on academic mentoring practices. Seek out these mentoring opportunities at your college campus or online via professional organizations. Such major conferences as the American Educational Research Association offer annual sessions that pair new faculty with outstanding scholars, sometimes seasoned editors, who are committed mentors. By getting to know such influential individuals, you may be able to overcome the intimidation that comes with refereed publishing and develop a relationship, even long-term, that serves your academic goals and interests.

In contrast, informal mentorship evolves spontaneously; these relationships are not assigned or monitored by the administration. When you initiate conversation with a faculty member who can help you with your scholarship and when you sustain that relationship, you have helped to create an informal mentorship. Research indicates that informal mentorships are more satisfying and productive for protégés and mentors alike, largely because mutual understanding, respect, and trust have the chance to evolve. You will probably find that experienced faculty are most receptive to mentoring new faculty who show strong academic promise and whose scholarly and/or professional interests are aligned with their own.

From a positive connection, reciprocity has a chance to develop, meaning that both parties can expect to benefit from the relationship. These gains are not just cognitive or career-focused, they are also psychosocial; excellent mentoring should affirm who you are and your values as a developing scholar. It is one thing to receive help in such areas as publication productivity and research presentations, but it is quite another to feel that you have earned the respect of a senior colleague. Through the kind of informal mentoring that enhances your well-being as a new scholar, your sense of competence, identity, and work-role effectiveness can all be expected to increase. Professional friendship, emotional intimacy, and authentic communication are payoffs for new faculty who establish truly meaningful scholarly relationships with faculty mentors.

In addition to the traditional individual mentor, you may also identify primary or secondary mentors for assistance. Secondary mentors often help in specific areas and compensate for weaknesses in the primary relationship. Identify those faculty who would make good secondary mentors largely because of the specialized knowledge or skill they can offer you. Maybe they are outstanding with respect to knowing the ins and outs of relevant journals and publishing presses in your discipline, or are particularly attuned to the grants arena, have the ability to respond constructively to something you have written, or have a thick networking circle and know the "right" people who can situate your work in important ways. Informational sources, peer readers, and accomplished networkers all make for excellent resources. Reach out and you will be surprised how many people will reach back to assist you.

Finally, why not join or establish multiple mentoring networks of scholars willing to help you and to learn from you? Catalytic productivity has been associated with viable writing support groups. Reports from the literature attest to the fact that numerous coauthored articles and other joint projects have materialized from synergistic groups. It can "take a village" to produce multiple publications, so why go at it alone? However, exercise caution: You do not want to experience death by mentoring or a loss of energy and focus. And remember: Undesirable interpersonal dynamics, incongruent expectations, or misguided conversations are all risk factors in academic mentorships.

46   WHEN SEEKING A WRITING MENTOR BE SELECTIVE

Choose productive academics to be your writing mentors. Very often, prolific writers are also prolific mentors. They find joy and excitement in the writing enterprise and enjoy teaching and learning with others. On the other hand, some highly productive academics make lousy mentors. They manifest disinterest, excessive self-focus, or poor interpersonal skills. Some may seem interested but then pull back out of sheer workload or overcommitment, while others are simply too cynical about the value of mentoring to be of any assistance. Find out for yourself which scholars are approachable, accessible, and relational—hopefully, some of these will be prolific academics or rising scholars with an inclination to mentor.

Here is the key: Choose carefully! Find out about the prolific faculty in your institution or field by doing your homework—who are they? What do they stand for? What have they accomplished? What do their colleagues and students say about them? What philosophical foundations underlie their published research? What are their research foci and interests, as evident by such documents as vitae and Web pages? And what about those individuals whom they have been helping? What light do current protégés have to shed?

Remember, the goal is to find productive academics who are responsive and who will give you time and energy. Consider seeking a mentoring relationship with someone suitable inside your department, college, or university, as well as scholars on the outside. Find people who share your research interests and with whom you can brainstorm about your writing goals and projects. Some new faculty strongly prefer mentoring from faculty who are similar in gender or race, while others have no such preference or even prefer cross-gender or -race relationships. Act on your personal needs when it comes to mentoring matches: Where desirable, contact minority or women's associations on your campus who may have insights about who might be the best mentor for you.

Even the most generous faculty, those with all the traits of excellent mentors, will hope for a two-way street when it comes to rewards. What can you offer mentors that will make their investment in you worthwhile, beyond the obvious payoff of intrinsic joy in helping a novice writer? If this consideration fails to ring true right now it is because novice writers tend to assume that seasoned scholars are naturally altruistic. Keep in mind that mentors are human; like any other long-term relationship, mentorships are most enjoyable when they develop informally and provide positive experiences for both partners. As another cautionary note, seasoned faculty often avoid newcomers who seem overly needy or self-serving. Keep in mind that faculty are not typically compensated for mentoring faculty or students, unless their mentorships have been formally recognized in their annual assignment of duties—a rare phenomenon in our experience.

What do you bring to the "mentoring table," then? You have lots of energy and enthusiasm, no doubt, and intriguing ideas and up-to-date information about your field. What are your scholarly strengths? Are you particularly good at searching academic databases, analyzing others' works, or brainstorming ideas, for example? Although we advocate reciprocity in mentorships, don't expect to be able to reciprocate immediately. And don't feel bad about this—when the time is right, think about ways to give back to your mentor.

Use writing mentors well. Excellent mentors may offer a meaningful collaboration resulting in gains in your scholarly sophistication and productivity. Expect an outstanding mentor to sponsor and validate you—both keys to your professional development. The most synergistic academic mentorships often generate numerous writing products in the form of papers, articles, and books. Further, many of these evolve into meaningful friendships over the long haul.

No matter the particular arrangement, an "N of 2" (you and your mentor) can help you to accomplish a great deal early in your career. Choose carefully. And once a mentor candidate emerges, take initiative for starting a collaboration, work to reciprocate when you can, and when a mentorship proves helpful, work to keep it active.

47   ACCESS WRITING COACHES
FOR SPECIFIC CONCERNS

Distinguish carefully between coaches and mentors in your selection of writing guides. Coaches are teachers or trainers who assist faculty by enabling the development of skills in specific areas. For example, a writing coach might help with organizational and grammatical structures, the art of editing and revising, or potentially good matches between manuscripts prepared for review and peer-reviewed journals. In contrast to mentorships, coaching does not assume a personal relationship. Whereas mentorships are typically long-term personal relationships concerned with your development as a scholar and person more broadly, coaching may be conceptualized as a short-term and focused consultative arrangement.

Coaches offer specialized assistance, generally for a fixed period and in response to specific needs, by helping with writing-related problems. Approach selected colleagues for focal coaching; seek consultation with respect to specific skills and problem solving. Coaches can be located through word-of-mouth or by searching your university directory or the Internet. Writing coaches may or may not be local and they can be faculty, administrators, staff, or for-hire editors working in the publishing industry—anyone experienced with the writing enterprise and capable of responding to your needs.

As mentioned, turn to collegial writing coaches to find out about the most fitting journals or outlets for your work. Even reference librarians can help with this task. Or, you may want tips on how best to approach publishers and their staff with your questions. Alternatively, it may be that you need access to contextual information (e.g., institutional ideals, practices, or values) to include in your writing project. Coaches can also help with identifying appropriate and timely material for your research, accessing sorely needed library sources and electronic databases, and much more. If you are struggling with some facet of writing, or have focused "how to" questions about the nuts and bolts of getting published, a coach—whether an informal colleague or a paid expert—may be just the ticket.

Quite often, talented coaches dwell deep within the infrastructure of higher education and often go practically unnoticed as treasure troves of knowledge and experience. Here are a few ideas about how to locate these diamonds in the rough. First, supervisory staff responsible for sponsored research programs at your campus process faculty applications every semester. They have intimate knowledge of what makes for a solid, competitive grant proposal. See if they might provide feedback on your work prior to the deadline. Also, the faculty development or instructional dean's office in your institution often houses experienced academicians who have made consulting with new faculty a forte. If they cannot provide direct guidance themselves, they can certainly point you in the direction of the right coach on campus. And here is another idea: Copyeditors who work for publishing companies can provide extensive, detailed feedback on papers-in-progress and, once again, know what makes for a successful piece of writing and how to help get you there.

Talented copyeditors will help bring out your important message so that you can communicate clearly and effectively on paper through such means as eliminating wordiness and side points, and streamlining academic jargon. The most experienced of copyeditors should be able to quickly detect and address areas of concern in your writing. Simply having a talented copyeditor mark up and edit a draft of your work can teach you more about writing than hours of didactic instruction. Learn from editors and work on your relative deficits by patiently revising your own writing. Writing clubs and communities of writers are other venues for connecting with potential coaches—these are often serious students of the art and craft of writing.

When seeking coaches for focused writing assistance, turn to informants in your department or institution. Informants will serve as indispensable connectors between you and the right coach. Deans, chairs, seasoned faculty, program coordinators, committee leaders, and others often know who the excellent coaches are. These academic connectors have access to a rich network of scholars.

Last, don't overlook your own capacity for writing self-help. Do you sometimes write in your head? Do you find yourself engaging in scholarly problem-solving during the day? If not, learn to deliberately process writing thoughts and project scenarios on a daily basis and make this a habit. Paul Thomas (2005), a scholar of writing, reflects on how, through our everyday mental states, we bring purpose and focus to our writing. Eating, talking, exercising, traveling, showering, and even dreaming can all provide excellent opportunities for coaching yourself on writing. As ideas spark during these daily (and nightly!) activities, record them in a journal or computer file, or on audiotape. Type or transcribe your jottings and give them coherence. Watch meaningful patterns of thought develop over time from this writing ritual. Don't wait for the perfect time and setting to write! Quite frankly, we're not certain that such a writing nirvana exists, at least not often. Key elements of many of our own publications—dissertations, books, and articles—emerged from insights captured while on the run. One of us ended up with a published article based on notes "scrawled" on a Starbucks napkin. Much can come from such humble beginnings.

48   USE MENTORS TO LEARN ACADEMIC CULTURAL NORMS

Prolific faculty use academic writing and work to decipher and understand the cultural context—including its pressures—that shape the writer's world. You will find that each institution has its own "personality"—cultural norms, unique history and mission, types of networks, values belonging to leaders and faculty, and idiosyncratic approaches to work. Count on a good mentor to serve as seasoned guide and willing informant as you master the norms governing the local writing milieu.

Faculty mentors have the capacity to offer salient institutional knowledge that encompasses the tenure-and-promotion process and other critical matters, namely cultural norms. New faculty who reach out to mentors and receive support are often better prepared along the road to tenure and promotion. They are also more inclined to stay at the same institution until tenure is achieved. Those without mentors are more prone to join tenure-track faculty who leave their initial positions without tenure, either moving onto tenure-earning positions elsewhere or moving into a nonacademic setting—by some estimates, as high as 50 percent of all tenure-track faculty (de Janasu & Sullivan, 2004).

In Payne's (1998) classic *A Framework for Understanding Poverty*, she describes the significance of human capital. Within the academy many of us, certainly new faculty, overemphasize the value of economic capital, while underestimating that of human capital. We are so focused on salaries and start-up funds that we forget to consider the availability of willing mentors. How many job seekers actually treat mentoring as a key resource and negotiate its terms as part of their acceptance of the position? If Payne is correct, then we all require support systems, relationships/role models, and knowledge of hidden rules to maintain our chances of success. Apply this to your own writing life: Who is available to help you with the complexities of learning the academic cultural norms in your institution and field?

Making good use of expert writing support and guidance should naturally translate into developing knowledge of the hidden rules that govern your workplace and discipline. Here's one such "hidden rule" bearing on scholarly writing: Scholars who refuse to make the changes that publishers ask of them or who do so only superficially appear to be dismissive of scholarly standards, which can cost them dearly.

Countless hidden rules shape one's success or failure in the academy. Collegiality, a human necessity, embodies at the relationship level many hidden rules. For example, the attitude one is *perceived* as bringing to the workplace may be crucial to your ultimate success. Just read the *Chronicle of Higher Education* to learn about the role that collegiality ostensibly plays in the tenure decisions made by departmental and college committees. While tenured faculty enjoy the luxury of staying at home to write whenever possible, different rules sometimes exist for tenure-earning faculty. Although we previously encouraged you to block out time and write from home when you can, remember that junior faculty must also make themselves visible around the office at times. Writing in a closeted fashion at work should not raise any eyebrows—at least you will be "present" and accounted for. If you will be working at home, it may be best to let your departmental chair or mentor know. Approach your department and college as an eager scholar who exhibits a professional attitude and leadership style. Get noticed. Through collaboration on writing projects and many other avenues (e.g., a limited number of committee assignments), you will be able to develop meaningful relationships with faculty and students. Stay positive in your interactions with faculty, mentors, and students, and reach out for advice. Forge a scholarly identity at your new institution that takes into account those around you: Learn how your scholarship fits and what you offer that is unique, and find ways to "market" yourself. You can give "brown bag" seminars or offer talks in colleagues' classes on your research.

Becoming a productive scholar means becoming intimately acquainted with the forces governing the academic cultural norms of faculty, students, and administrators. Turn to faculty mentors and respected others in-the-know to learn about the cultural norms that will influence your scholarship.

49   NOT ALL WRITERS BENEFIT FROM MENTORING, NETWORKING, AND COACHING

We conclude this chapter on mentoring, coaching, and networking by acknowledging that not everyone requires or stands to benefit from writing consultations and writing-focused relationships. Here are the most common reasons why new academics might eschew writing assistance.

Many academics—including new hires fresh from graduate school—are dyed-in-the-wool introverts. Several strands of research on personality traits and types among college professors confirm a consistent propensity toward fierce independence; as a group, many among us are shy, driven, and given to seeking solitude. There are several reasons why introverts might be attracted to careers in academia, not the least of which is the opportunity for quiet and independent study. How does an introvert get rejuvenated and invigorated? Simple, he or she closes the office door. An undergraduate professor we know—a stellar teacher and classic introvert—had a doormat outside his office that queried would-be visitors: *Is this visit really necessary?* Blinds, photos, cartoons, and favorite quotes covering glass panes on faculty office doors are common privacy-protecting "graffiti." If you are an introvert, you are not alone in the academy!

Academics are harried. Pressed with overwhelming job demands, the prospect of giving up precious time to attend a networking meeting or have lunch with a potential mentor might seem noxious. No matter how you slice it, getting support and assistance with your writing takes some initial time commitment. Even extroverted academics might worry that giving up time for coaching and networking will be about as beneficial or exciting as attending a faculty meeting.

But there can be deeper reasons for avoiding assistance that merit honest reflection. Some of us may be rigidly independent because we distrust others or expect to be exploited. Some of us are so insecure about our status in academe that we avoid help-seeking for fear of being revealed as an intellectual imposter. Some academics harbor such anemic self-esteem that they anticipate being undone by critical feedback. Still others are prone to shame at revealing their inner worlds to strangers; they have been conditioned to see the act of writing as something done in private. Finally, many of us were never afforded the opportunity to view ourselves as serious writers or to live the writer's life. It may therefore be difficult to see ourselves as legitimate members of any writer's community or to conceive of collaborative writing as an opportunity for skill development and growth.

Whatever a neophyte academic's rationale for avoiding help-seeking or collaboration, we encourage sober consideration of the potential drawbacks. Here are the primary concerns with not availing yourself of good mentoring, coaching, and networking when these might prove useful. First, academics who lack superb writing motivation and technical skill may simply be placing themselves at a disadvantage—both in regard to peers who do sharpen their writing acumen, and in regard to achieving a track record of scholarly success prior to the tenure-and- promotion hurdle. Second, a new faculty member who eschews help and assistance may become too isolated, not benefiting from the wisdom and support of wise mentors and willing colleagues. Of course, this may paradoxically diminish satisfaction with one's very career and work setting. Third, even relatively confident academics might inadvertently undermine their own self-esteem and self-efficacy. Remember, mentors, coaches, and colleagues are there to praise your work—not just criticize it! Finally, the exclusively solo writer might miss out on opportunities for accelerating productivity through collaborative projects and writing teams. Regardless of your discipline, coauthored works do count toward promotion; when you find the right collaborator(s), it is frequently possible to double or triple your output by contributing to a team effort. And, along the way, you are likely to learn a thing or two about more effective writing.

Having explored the common reasons for not seeking or engaging senior faculty, writing experts, and peers, we now return to the title of this section: Not all writers benefit from mentoring, coaching, and networking. There is no shame in writing alone. If you have no concern about any of the potential drawbacks noted previously, if you strongly prefer to learn about writing through trial and error, and, more important, if you are both writing efficiently and getting good responses from publishers, then we see no reason why mentoring, coaching, or networking are imperative. Just don't get too lonely!

9

TACKLE THOUGHTS AND
EMOTIONS THAT
BLOCK PRODUCTIVITY

Emotions can be both powerful drivers and blockers in our productivity as scholars. In this chapter we consider writing-related emotions and cognitions from different perspectives. We emphasize avenues for correcting those that threaten to slow or block your writing. Neophyte scholars need to work especially hard at getting past irrational thoughts that interfere with writing. Self-defeating and counterproductive thoughts and behaviors are worsened by negative drama-making about one's scholarly plights. No doubt, procrastination is the writer's enemy: Overcome the tendency to stall productive work by making a commitment to write every day and by confronting any unconscious factors enabling procrastinating behavior. Reinforcing desired behaviors helps with these goals. Create pleasurable or satisfying connections to writing by rewarding yourself in deliberate, planned ways. We share some of our own reinforcing techniques. Develop your resilience as a writer so that you will have the ability to deal with rejections and the disappointment that naturally accompanies them. We provide techniques for maintaining perspective in the face of publishing setbacks and share how resilient academics and prolific authors overcome these inevitable hurdles. After all is said and done, you are a writer, writing is not you. Maintain varied life interests if you want to function as a well-adjusted, multifaceted college professor; faceting will enhance resilience in the face of adversity.

50   Dispute Thoughts
that Interfere with Writing

Far too many fledgling writers sabotage themselves from the start with a striking propensity toward *irrational beliefs* about themselves, about their writing, and about other members of the writing community (e.g., reviewers, colleagues, editors). Famous clinical psychologist Albert Ellis (1985) observed that all human beings—college professors being no exception—can be talented neurotics, that is prone to blocking their own progress and disturbing themselves with very little help from the outside world. Each of us is prone to at least episodic struggles with irrational beliefs: Such beliefs are illogical, unsupported by data, and nearly always self-defeating and counterproductive. Irrational beliefs frequently lead not only to problem behaviors (e.g., stymied writing, procrastination, tirades against editors), but, more often, self-defeating emotions (e.g., depression, anxiety, anger, and shame).

As writers, most of us hold strong preferences, wishes, and desires relative to our scholarship. Here are some from our own experience: (1) I wish that writing would always be fun and that I had plenty of discretionary time to devote to it; (2) I'd prefer it if reviewers would always be enthralled with my work and prone to recommend publication with very little revision; (3) I'd really like it if the editors of top journals would accept my work straightaway the first time it was submitted. What's wrong with these preferences? Nothing! As long as they remain preferences and wishes, there is little chance any of these will cause significant upset or disturbance. The real problem, however, is that in some cases, we don't confine these notions to preferences. Instead, our imagination transforms them into absolute demands. Any time a preference escalates to a dire necessity, watch out!—this is a recipe for disturbed emotions and disordered behavior that directly inhibit prolific work, as well as healthy relationships.

According to Ellis (1985), three primary types of irrational thinking potentially undergird our emotional upsets: (1) *demands* (unrealistic and absolutistic expectations of events or individuals that are recognizable by key words such as "must," "should," or "ought"), (2) *catastrophizing* (exaggerating the negative consequence of a situation to an extreme degree), and (3) *global evaluation* (making extreme evaluations about the worth or value of self or others).

For a writer, any of these irrational beliefs can lead directly to self-defeating behavior and emotions. While reading the following examples, ask yourself whether you have fallen prey to any of these pernicious though common scholarly irrationalities.

- I *must* be successful in getting all of my work accepted for publication.
- I *ought to* be an outstanding scholar, clearly better than other writers and professors in my department, university, or discipline.
- I *have to* be greatly respected and loved by colleagues and editors.
- If a reviewer or editor caustically denigrates my work or rejects me, he or she is obviously *worthless* and should be removed from the position of power.
- If a reviewer or editor caustically denigrates my work or rejects me, it just proves that I am *worthless* and will always fail.
- I *should* find writing easy and enjoyable like other scholars in my college and field.
- If the audience at a professional conference should react negatively to my paper, it would be *catastrophic*—so *awful* I would probably vomit, faint, and be barred from ever attending the conference again.

Perhaps none of these common writer's beliefs ring true for you. Or, if you are like us, a few of them remind you of bleak moods or bouts of either self-deprecation or rage that followed a perceived failure or setback in your scholarly work. Of course, catalytic events (e.g., rejection letter, negative reviews, disgruntled audience) themselves have little power to "cause" emotional upset. Rather, it is our own human tendency to move from wishes and desires to absolutistic demands that turns unwanted events into dysfunctional behavior and affect.

In order to genuinely succeed as a prolific scholar, you *must* combat and overcome any tendency toward the irrational. If you are to prevent these widespread irrational thoughts from waylaying your work, you must actively dispute them. Refuse to catastrophize about anything—remember, it could *always* be worse; maintain unconditional self-acceptance no matter what others say about your work; and be on guard for demanding absolutes—crazy beliefs that serve only to cause upset. Work at disputing thoughts that interfere with writing and your own development and status as a writer using whatever creative means are at your disposal—constructive self-talk therapy, conversation with positive-minded individuals, and relevant self-help books, novels, and films are all examples of proactive strategies.

51   Overcome Procrastination or Die Trying

Just as cancer is insidious, malignant, and deadly to the human body, procrastination is dangerous to an academic's aspirations of scholarly success and institutional promotion. Think of procrastination as a writing (or rather nonwriting) syndrome that afflicts many new professors—and more than a few who are seasoned. In some cases, procrastination is overt and apparent (e.g., organizing files and cleaning one's desk when your office is already more organized than any obsessive-compulsive's, checking e-mail every five minutes, trying to construct a miniature Eiffel Tower from pretzels on your desk). But procrastination is more likely to be subtle and insidiously additive. Most of us, if honest, can easily identify minutes, and even hours each day that have been squandered on idle activity entirely unrelated to furthering one's status as scholar or teacher. These minutes, hours, and days are irretrievable!

Cognitive psychologists are rather blunt regarding the etiology of procrastination (Walen, DiGiuseppe, & Dryden, 1992). In a nutshell, the translation of procrastination is *laziness*. When we put off doing something that would be much better done today, it is often because our internal dialogue goes something like, "it's too hard," which actually means "unacceptably hard."

Let's face it, human beings are biologically and psychologically predisposed to pain-avoidance; when possible, all of us naturally prefer to forgo discomfort. But here is the rub: Many of the key elements and crucial moments of writing are inherently unpleasant and difficult—they demand that we bear down and "just do it," particularly when we don't feel like it. Most of us can easily recall days when getting the writing done meant foregoing something much more enjoyable and sacrificing our own comfort; all of us have days when nearly anything else seems more fun than writing (including cleaning our house or undergoing a root canal).

You may not be surprised to learn that Ellis (1985) identified a specific and pernicious irrational belief that often leads directly to procrastinating behavior among writers. He called it *Low Frustration Tolerance* (LFT), or discomfort intolerance. Any time we tell ourselves that we just "can't stand to do it," we are wallowing in LFT. The logical, empirical, and pragmatic reality is that we absolutely can, and in most circumstances had better *stand it* if we want to become prolific academics. When we move beyond a healthy truth such as "exerting the effort required to get back on track and make some writing headway may be both difficult and unpleasant," and add an irrational evaluation of this truth such as "and it would be excruciating and unbearable, I just can't do it," we are likely to procrastinate.

Procrastination has the same quality as quicksand in the life of a scholar. The more writing days you miss, the farther you get from your own work, the colder it begins to feel on cognitive and emotional levels, and the more effort it will require to get back in the groove again. Think of this procrastination-as-quicksand principle as a form of negative inertia. During the middle of writing this book, one of your authors sustained a shoulder injury. Although there was little pain involved, during the ensuing months range of motion declined radically—the author was favoring and restricting the shoulder's use on a completely unconscious level. By the time significant pain developed, a syndrome called "frozen shoulder" had developed and a lengthy and painful trial of physical therapy was required to break the tendon free of the bones to which it had adhered through disuse. We think that frozen shoulder might be an apt metaphor for procrastination. Before you develop "frozen writing" syndrome, pay attention to early signs of procrastination, avoidance, and decreasing productivity. It is imperative that you force yourself to do the work, devote the time, and exercise your writing tools often.

Although we believe that the lion's share of procrastination can be attributed to the LFT and intolerance for discomfort, we recognize that avoiding writing can also be a visible symptom of a latent conflict. Without treading into psychoanalysis, we do acknowledge that procrastination can also signal fear of success (self-defeating behavior), ambivalence about an academic career (failure to prepare effectively for promotion and tenure provides a way out of an unwanted vocation), or even unresolved opposition to authority—all unconscious processes. If you find yourself frequently struggling with procrastination and if it appears to be more than just LFT, then seeking some professional consultation might be necessary.

Is there an antidote to procrastination? For starters, return to chapter one in this guide and reread each component in establishing a well-honed writing habit. This section should reawaken a commitment to write every day—even when you just don't feel like it. If LFT is your Achilles heal, then each day as you prepare to buckle down, close your door, and write, adopt a mantra such as "I *can* stand it and I *will!*" Other specific tips include posting updated checklists, making daily sacrifices such as bringing lunch to work instead of joining colleagues, warding off distracters in your environment, and telling a colleague or loved one your plan, so you can be reminded to get the work done. By combating LFT and confronting any unconscious factors enabling your procrastinating behavior, procrastination should become more transparent and distasteful; discomfort intolerance should become a less potent motivator. And consequently, you should find that you are able to push through the temptation to procrastinate and get back to being productive.

52   Reinforce Desired Behaviors

In the psychology of learning, the *law of effect* states that those responses or behaviors in any situation that are accompanied or closely followed by satisfaction will be more firmly connected to that situation, so that when it recurs, those responses and behaviors will also be likely to recur. What does this "boring" principle have to do with you as a writer? If you can manage to create pleasurable or satisfying connections to your writing, it is likely that writing will become a higher-frequency behavior. So, if the situation at hand involves a two-hour block of time during your day, and the behavior you engage in is diligent scholarship, it will help if you can find a way of making the experience pleasurable—either by making the work itself enjoyable, or by overtly reinforcing yourself for a job well done.

We strongly advocate for the use of positive reinforcement to increase the consistency and volume of your writing, and to enhance your sense of well-being. Decades of research confirms that famous American psychologist B. F. Skinner was right after all: Desired behaviors must be shaped and rewarded if we want them to increase in frequency. Even the most sophisticated and intellectual among us will work more effectively if small pleasures and delightful respites are scheduled into what can be an otherwise grinding task. To reinforce is to fortify, strengthen, augment, or buttress; we reinforce any behavior when we apply a reward or experience that increases the probability that the behavior will reoccur. So, making highly preferred activities contingent upon planned writing activity can work wonders, especially for anyone who associates writing strictly with hard work.

If you are a cynic about the potential benefits of deliberate self-reinforcement for your own writing, let us share some examples of reinforcement from our own writing lives. In order to make the experience of writing itself rewarding (and less like the experience of a rat on a wheel), one of us closes the door and brews a fresh pot of gourmet coffee. The chair and keyboard are adjusted for maximal comfort, and some planning occurs for using the time available to maximize gain. If the task at hand is working on references or scanning previous literature, a click of the mouse brings up some light jazz for an enjoyable auditory background. To make writing pleasurable, the other author hunkers down in her chamber of silence with some green tea and writes scholarly "to-dos" on post-its, discarding each one as the task is completed, and continuing until none are left at the end of the evening. Music and sounds are disruptive to this author, but visual stimuli are most welcoming, with a budding hibiscus tree and surrounding potscape garden planted directly outside the home office window. You get the idea: By making the writing experience itself rewarding, we find that we are more likely to enjoy the experience, and more willing to comply with our writing schedule each day.

But reinforcement also requires the application of reward following the desired response. Therefore, when we complete a sizable writing block, or more important, when we wrap up a journal or book manuscript, we are careful about intentionally rewarding ourselves. Some of our favorite reinforcements for being productive include a long run or walk along the water or golf course, an afternoon off to play with kids, a luncheon with favorite colleagues, taking in a movie with a friend, an elegant meal out or a barbecue feast at home, relaxing with a novel or some other pleasure reading (and napping), or even taking a day-trip to a beach resort, possibly staying overnight at a bed-and-breakfast. We often find that deciding on reinforcement ahead of time is quite useful; keeping the desired reward in sight during the hard work serves as a delightful stimulus to endurance and forbearance of discomfort along the way. But remember that reinforcements are idiosyncratic. Not all readers will think of jogging or fiction reading as rewards—they are likely to be noxious activities to some! So, pick nourishing rewards that are truly reinforcing for you and make them contingent upon doing the work.

What about punishment? Some behavior therapists strongly encourage the application of both reinforcement (for desired behaviors) and punishment (for those behaviors you wish to extinguish). Although punishment can be quite effective at times, remember that reinforcement is usually better in the long run, and that excessive punishment can lead to learned help-lessness, shame, and stagnation. If you do decide to apply pun-ishments to behavior such as procrastination and failure to engage in the prescribed writing each day, try things that have a humorous flavor. For example, if you fail to complete your scheduled writing block, decide in advance that you must clean your house that evening, flush five dollars down the toilet, or engage in 15 minutes of idle chatter with your least favorite colleague or neighbor. You get the idea, make punishments noxious (not dangerous) and force yourself to follow through if you want them to have maximal effect at reducing the frequency of undesired behaviors.

Remember the law of effect and increase the frequency of desired behaviors through the judicious use of thoughtful reinforcements. Treat yourself right as a writer; you are worth it.

53   REFUSE TO DWELL ON SETBACKS

Here is an interesting fact about prolific writers: Almost without exception, they are characterized by and are models of *resilience*. Because nearly every academic will have his or her share of rejection, because acceptance rates for most journals and grant competitions are quite low, and because schedules, students, and colleagues consistently "conspire" to thwart productivity, the capacity for resilience in the face of adversity is a salient predictor of success as a scholar. Resilience as a writer suggests a certain attitude of equanimity and calm even when faced with dramatic disappointment. Resilience indicates the ability to take setbacks in stride, to stay relatively unruffled, and to respond adaptively, doggedly, and repeatedly until goals are achieved.

Upon submitting scholarly work for peer review, it is imperative that one should expect rejection from editors and publishers. Rejection comes with the scholarly writing territory—it is one of its most prominent landscape marks. The fact is that not experiencing setbacks in the form of rejections, delays, and disappointments would be quite atypical—maybe even bizarre. You'd have license to star in your own movie about space aliens or unknown worlds! Even if you are an excellent thinker and careful writer, you should expect many of your submissions to be rejected. And you should expect many more to be hung up in what may feel like an endless cycle of reviews and resubmissions to the same journal. You must expect lengthy and aggravating delays in the review process because reviewers are late and editors are often slow to make decisions, sometimes for reasons outside their immediate control, such as holiday periods, tardy reviewers, and leadership turnover. You should also expect that busy students and well-intended colleagues will be late with their drafts and contributions to joint projects and that they will occasionally disappoint you with subpar work. And of course you can anticipate that your personal life will intrude when you least expect or desire it—sick children, infirm parents, personal injury or health issues, and financial stressors can all push back against your best-laid plans for writing.

So how can you refuse to dwell on these nearly certain setbacks on the road to becoming prolific? First, avoid catastrophic reactions to bad news or unwelcome periods when you cannot write. The prolific writer masters a sort of Zen contemplative attitude to these events—evaluating them objectively without creating drama or emotional upset. Kicking your computer down the stairs, burning a letter from an editor, or going on a drinking binge are all obvious indicators that your equanimity has faltered. But there are more subtle indicators of pathologic reaction to setbacks. Some of us are prone to stewing and ruminating about rejections or disappointments. Rather than take negative feedback in stride, we become obsessively preoccupied with the "injustice" against ourselves and engage in the kinds of irrational thinking covered earlier in this chapter—we demand, we self-disparage, and we engage in low frustration tolerance. If you are prone to moody brooding in the wake of editorial rejection, ask yourself how you reach this point. Sometimes rumination comes from narcissistic injury (e.g., "how dare the editor fail to admire the brilliance of my work"), and sometimes it stems from depressive thinking (e.g., "I knew my work was worthless—this just proves it"). But whatever the etiology, the outcome is emotional disturbance and procrastination.

How do resilient academics and prolific authors overcome setbacks? First of all, they reframe rejection as an opportunity to learn more about writing well, to improve the quality of the rejected manuscript, and as a chance to submit their work to another outlet that may in fact be a better match. Quite often, prolific scholars put rejection letters and accompanying reviews away for a few days, collect their thoughts, and then read them with a deliberate and an objectively detached attitude that allows honest and productive responses to the feedback. Of course, prolific scholars also work hard at refusing to exacerbate the situation by stewing or engaging in self-defeating behaviors (e.g., writing snide letters back to editors, shredding their work, refusing to make necessary revisions in the manuscript, succumbing to emotional downward spiraling).

In some ways, successful writers are like the "Energizer bunny" from the famous battery commercial. They just keep on writing and keep on submitting their work until they improve their own writing, become skilled at the mechanics of manuscript preparation, become well-versed in the art of interacting with editors, and eventually begin to achieve better than average success with publication. Prolific scholars hone the gifts of tenacity and fortitude. And they just keep on going!

54   YOU ARE A WRITER, WRITING IS NOT YOU

Throughout this guide, we have pushed you to make writing a top priority, both in your career, and in the rhythm of each day. Prolific scholars make the act of writing a pervasive part of their lives and an essential element of their scholarly identities. But there is a rub. It can be quite tempting for academics to allow their self-esteem to hinge on publishing success; they may unwittingly allow writing to become the only important dimension in their lives. If number or prestige of publications is the sole, or even the primary, indicator of your success as a human being, or even as a professor, chances are you are allowing performance as a writer to hold too much sway in defining who you are.

To achieve happiness as a scholar, it is imperative that you recognize—hopefully early on—that writing is only one facet of an academic life well lived. In the end, most of your publications will merely be lines on a vita. Although all of us would like many such entries on the vita, only a few of us will write works that go on to significantly influence our fields for decades, let alone centuries. In reality, most of what you write today will be ignored or all but forgotten even before you reach the end of your career. This is the bitter truth for most of us. Put your writing in perspective. It should be a very exciting and rewarding element of your life and career, but it should never become your only focus. Practice humility: Feel fortunate to even be read or appreciated for your writing by any of your students, colleagues, and contemporaries.

In our experience, scholars with a wide range of life interests and time investments are better adjusted and more resilient in the face of adversity. When life contains more than a single facet—when your world revolves around more than just lines on the vita—you are said to be *multifaceted* (Johnson & Ridley, 2004), and this is good. All things considered, multifaceted college professors are likely to maintain better health and a more realistic perspective when frustration, disappointment, and failure strike. Those colleagues who work to ensure that prolific writing is but one facet of their identities seem more capable of avoiding catastrophic reactions to rejection—they learn to value and pursue scholarship while keeping it in perspective.

How can you work toward ensuring your own faceting? Ask yourself how often you invest time in family, important relationships outside of work, physical exercise, recreational pursuits, and personal hobbies. Are these things too frequently sacrificed at the altar of productivity? Or when you are engaged in nonwork pursuits, are you unable to really enjoy them due to preoccupation with a research conundrum or frustration at not working? Does your laptop need to be within reach at all times in order for you to have peace of mind? Although we risk invoking a well-worn cliché here, we think it is probably accurate that very few college professors reach the end of their lives grieving about their lack of productivity or stewing about those manuscripts they didn't get written. No. More scholars who experience any regret at the end may wonder why they ignored everything but productivity. Cherish your life in the living of it—don't expect writing alone to give meaning to it.

Think carefully about your own life-priority balancing act. Are you disciplined and no-nonsense about getting the writing done while still saving precious time for relationships and other interests? If not, find ways to move yourself in this direction. Here is an existential exercise to help you reflect on your current faceting: Imagine that tomorrow your ability to write was removed—never again could you produce scholarship. How well would you cope? Would you effectively cease to exist? Is your identity comprised of more than your stature or performance as a scholar? After grieving the loss of this cherished activity, could you reorient and begin focusing more actively on other current interests, relationships, and pressing matters? These are thought-provoking and maybe difficult questions. Ask and answer them honestly. They should help to illuminate your current faceting status.

10

Master the Mechanics of Publication: What Publishers Want You to Know

Although we have touched upon the importance of the mechanics of publication elsewhere in this book, because of its salience we devote here an entire chapter to its particularities. Put aside any embarrassment you may feel, and solicit feedback from peer readers and proofreaders on your works-in-progress—especially those that will be juried. Astute readers see what even very good writers cannot about their texts, and crucial areas of improvement can always be identified in neophytes' writings. Make good use of skilled readers *before* you submit your work for publishing review, especially if you are a junior faculty member or a student. Target your manuscript to a specific journal or publisher by finding out which are the first- and second-tier journals or publishers in your field. Also learn the acceptance rates for the various journals in which you will be submitting work. Find out about any special issues to which you might contribute your work. You will want to thoughtfully prepare your manuscripts by closely following the notes to authors and by giving yourself an incubation period before sending off your work for review. Carefully prepare your author's cover letter; if your work is accepted with modification, treat seriously the summary of changes that addresses the editor's recommendations and the reviewers' concerns. When you prepare a book prospectus, again, closely adhere to the publisher's submission guidelines and also communicate with the acquisitions editor. You will soon discover that marketing considerations are paramount in the development and review of proposals for books.

55 SOLICIT FEEDBACK FROM PEER READERS AND PROOFREADERS

Speaking as journal editors, editorial board members, journal and book authors, and manuscript reviewers, we know that getting your work through the peer-review gauntlet and into print can seem arduous, and that the publishing stakes are high when you are the author! To help ensure your progress and success as a published author, solicit the help of peer readers. Even the most outrageously prolific scholars seek feedback from talented colleagues. Consider leading educational scholar John Goodlad's approach to peer readers—he actively elicits feedback on drafts of his writing from contributors and coauthors. As one of his coauthors in the teacher education field attested, "He asks us for our reactions" and gives critical feedback, knowing that "friends don't flatter—enemies flatter" (Mullen, 2006, p. 13).

Writing is one thing, but publishing is quite another, and "the added elements of publishing changes the work of the writer" (Thomas, 2005, p. 114). Consideration of craft and audience are paramount in the publishing world, and these are learned skills. By craft we mean the ability to plan, make, or execute a work, and by audience we refer to one's anticipated and/or actual readers. Journal editors receive too many poorly constructed works. Many now ask that authors work with critical readers and excellent proofreaders before they submit their manuscripts for review; some recommend that this engagement with professional colleagues occur again after the work has been revised and prior to resubmission. Take this advice seriously, as the quality of the writing is, according to many editors, what makes or breaks a work submitted for review. Nothing says incompetence or carelessness to an editor like sloppy writing, typos, mismatched references, and other easily avoidable errors. Peer readers should be able to catch errors that bypass careful spell-checks and proofreading. Further, accomplished writers can make a substantive contribution to your text. They can identify needed improvement in such important areas as conceptualization and framing, research design and execution, and methodologies and results.

No matter how good you may feel about what you have written, and no matter how many times you may have read and improved upon your work, it is common to miss what a good reader can catch. Because others are not as emotionally invested in the work or tied closely to the outcome of the review process, they bring a fresh and honest set of lenses. Put your ego in the drawer and pull out your inquisitive learning self for this part of your journey. Lower your defenses: Be prepared to accept sound criticism and, over time, grow into being your own best critic. Become your own best editor too. The objective is to learn to trust your own editing and revising. Remember that there are no good writers, only good rewriters. Revise, revise, and revise some more: Return to your writing after a few days' break so that you will be refreshed and ready to see the work anew. Submit only your most polished work to publishers.

Successful publishing in academic outlets requires a steep learning curve: Even when manuscripts are well-written pieces that address important topics, they can suffer from problems of "match" with the idiosyncratic style and preferences of individual journals and editors. It is helpful when your proofreader is familiar with your intended outlet and can offer pinpointed stylistic advice. For example, your well-written paper may be insufficiently substantiated or lack relevant sources. Or, your work may be based on opinions with little data or literature to support them while your target journal is scrupulous about referencing. Depending upon the type of journal, successful manuscripts may require a larger subject pool and extensive analysis of data, as well as profound or original insights.

Seek answers to your questions from informed mentors and peers, scholarly guides, writing workshops, and legitimate Internet sources. And stay open to the questions that others may have of your work. It is profoundly self-defeating to solicit expert peer review and proofreading only to become defensive or argumentative when potential problems are revealed.

And don't forget to reciprocate: Act as a peer reader for your own peer readers. Be liberal with expressions of gratitude for the work of your peers, and when appropriate formally acknowledge others' contributions to your works directly within the texts themselves. Collaborative behaviors such as these will build the professional community of writers that define the academy and your own place within it.

56   TARGET YOUR MANUSCRIPT TO A SPECIFIC JOURNAL OR PUBLISHER

Decide where you will submit your paper for review before or during its preparation. Avoid making this decision on the day the work is being prepared for mailing. In some cases, you will already be familiar with the noteworthy journals in your area of scholarship. If not, it is wise to solicit input from faculty mentors and prolific scholars in your discipline. Ask them about the best outlets for your manuscripts. Those who have published in the journals you have in mind are particularly good resources. Who better to enlighten you about each journal's editorial and selection process, credibility, and normal time lag until publication? If they have recently published in the journal you are interested in, ask to see the rating form that the editor uses so that you will know how best to conform your own work to the journal's expectations. You can also ask editors for their forms directly, but some may be reluctant to provide them.

Also search for potential journals and style guidelines for authors specific to them using academic search engines that house mega-databases (e.g., Lexis Nexis, ProQuest, Wilson's Omni-File) and electronic venues that publish articles. Because each database has unique search methods, and because your search for specific journals will not always yield what you want to find, you may find it necessary to turn to a reference librarian or another qualified party for help. Try the Educational Resources Information Center (ERIC) Clearinghouse for up-to-date databases of journals and education literature (website: http://www.eric.ed.gov). Journals, complete with relevant publishing details, can also be located via the *Cabell's Dictionary* in your subject field (e.g., curriculum or psychology).

Find out the acceptance rates of relevant journals before you decide, and keep track of these in a file for tenure and promotion. Glatthorn (1998) recommends that beginners may want to submit their first manuscript to "less-selective" journals that publish a high number of those received. But consider whether this makes good sense for you. Some new scholars produce manuscripts that would be competitive in top-tier journals. Once again, this is where an experienced peer reviewer in your field could prove invaluable. Also decide whether you want to target a state, national, or international journal—each carries a different weight, with national refereed journals typically the most highly valued. Learn what journals and publishing presses have the greatest value in your own discipline and make decisions based on a whole host of variables that include the audience for your work, acceptance rates, and estimated time for the review.

Early in your academic career, it is frequently important to "prime the pump," so to speak, by getting some of your work published—even in second-tier journals. This affords you crucial experience with the peer review process, bolsters confidence, and allows you to establish a portfolio of publications before narrowing your list of target journals to the most competitive titles in your field. You might also consider taking advantage of electronic journals—some have higher acceptance rates than printed journals and are therefore less competitive; further, these outlets offer the benefits of speed, distribution, lengthier texts, flexible and artistic formats, and sometimes even dialogue with readers. On the downside, unless prestigious, electronic journals will hold less sway with most tenure-and-promotion committees.

Special issues of journals are certainly worth targeting—especially when the topic dovetails with your own scholarly focus or interests. Examples of special issue topics in education that have been published in recent years include reconceptualizing leadership, school improvement, and preparation; mentoring and technology: exploring the nexus; and teacher activism in education reform. Special issues are announced far in advance through the websites of journals, hard copy journals, and flyers distributed via professional associations. Word-of-mouth is another way that academics find out about such publishing opportunities. The acceptance rate is generally higher for these than regular issues of journals (Henson, 1999). As another point, because special issues feature works on similar or related topics, new faculty can contact the other authors appearing in the issue to plant seeds for future collegial collaboration, mentorship, and coauthorship. This action will serve to broaden your network and knowledge of who is currently contributing to your area of research.

Read and study the journals you are interested in—avoid submitting blindly, hoping for a fit. Outright rejections are common, so try to avoid this time-waster. Of course if the publication is new and no issues are available for you to read, you will need to adopt a different strategy: Contact the editors with your response to their call for papers and stimulate a dialogue around the potential fit of your work with the journal's scope, goals, and purpose. For established journals, read articles appearing in their current, not just past, issues. Analyze their content, style, organization, diction, and everything relevant to articles the editor has recently published. Adopt big questions for orienting yourself to the material. As one example, you might be interested in learning whether the published pieces are more qualitatively or quantitatively oriented, or whether the authors are writing in the first or third person.

After you have made a careful assessment, ask yourself whether the journal you have selected is an appropriate choice for the work you are developing (or plan to write). While the topic and focus of your paper may fit, important aspects such as the method, style, and length may not. Be soberly analytical regarding the goodness-of-fit. On those occasions when the match remains unclear, contact the journal editor directly and be forthcoming with your questions. Share your abstract, if possible, and outline your questions or dilemma. Ask whether the journal is a good place for your work and, if not, whether a recommendation can be made for another journal. Editors make excellent critics, many are genuinely supportive, and most are established, even leading, authors in their disciplines. More and more editors are even electronically "previewing" entire texts online, letting authors know whether the work fits and, if so, what else needs to be done to get it ready for external review. Clearly, all such coaching moves can only help academics to better position themselves as published authors whose productivity reveals a regular, if not impressive, pattern.

Finally, volunteer to review for the journals in your area of academic interest and accept invitations to review manuscripts that could serve to forward your writing/research agenda by extending your knowledge. Reviewing manuscripts will certainly help you become intimately informed regarding expectations for publication in journals in your field; it will also help you to become a better, more astute writer.

57   CAREFULLY PREPARE YOUR MANUSCRIPT

In order to significantly increase the probability of getting your work into print, literally and assiduously follow the published submission guidelines of journals and book publishers. Submission guidelines are available in printed issues of journals or online at websites. In our experiences as editors, authors commonly overlook some or even most elements of a journal's submission guidelines. Beware: Some editors ignore manuscripts that do not conform to their published expectations—these are not returned. Typical problems encompass not only the formatting of the actual paper but also the number of review copies requested, insufficient information on the identifying title page (such as electronic and fax addresses), and more. Of course, electronic submissions of papers, which are increasingly popular, eliminate the need for copies and change some other normative practices, such as the signed cover letter. Create your own submission checklist using the guidelines provided for each publisher selected.

If an editor should request a file copy on disk to aid with the review process, be sure to include it. An editor we know says that he can tell that an author has not read his journal's guidelines if they have *included* an abstract, as the guidelines explicitly state that abstracts will not be reviewed or published. Authors who fail to include the requisite number of copies for review purposes or who do not prepare "blind" copies (if requested) may not have their work reviewed either. Blind copies retain your anonymity and the fair treatment of your work during the review process; copies prepared for blind review do not have the author's name in the manuscript or in the references. Here is the message: Don't make assumptions about what an outlet or an editor expects.

As you consult a journal's submission guidelines, you may notice that they frequently vary from one journal to another. Journal guidelines in education typically require American Psychological Association (APA) formatted papers—as of 2006 the fifth edition is current. The *Chicago Manual of Style* for humanities and social science professors and the Modern Language Association (MLA) for English professors are the other widely known styles that publishers expect prospective authors to use. Be sure to look closely for any deviations from the norm. If an in-house style is used, make the required adjustments. Typically, publishers will specify on a style sheet any variations to be adopted, especially for citations and references—this request, typical of international publishers such as Routledge/Taylor & Francis Group is often outlined on Websites. Be sure not to format your paper merely by using the published "look" of the journal. An article's printed appearance may not accurately reflect the journal's submission requirements or the desired manuscript format.

Granted, the documentation styles (APA, Chicago, MLA) are not easy to learn—it takes years of practice. Many of us who know them well still have to refer to the guides to refresh our memories or to clarify one of the many daunting rules, such as proper electronic citation. We recommend that in addition to using the latest version of a formatting manual, you access a user-friendly guide and share it with students.

For blind review processes, provide two different title pages. On the author identifying page, include the manuscript title, as well as your complete address and contact information (a functioning e-mail address is essential). For the blind copies of your paper, provide only the title on the first page. To emphasize: Authors should not count on extra work being done on their behalf and so should take the necessary steps to submit complete packages. (Using a graduate student or secretary for this purpose is not, generally speaking, a good idea.) Where an abstract is required, be sure it adheres to the stipulated word length and is arranged as a single block paragraph. Your papers must also fall within the maximum word length. Not all journals clarify a maximum, so ask the editor. For research articles, the abstract usually covers the essential elements of the paper—topic, purpose and scope, methods and data analysis, the insights or findings yielded, and the primary significance or implications. These are also highlighted in some form as headings throughout the paper. For international journals, editors expect to see relevance beyond your state or country, so give this some careful thought, perhaps in the implications section of your paper.

Again, avoid submitting unnecessarily lengthy manuscripts for review. Unless the contribution is truly monumental in importance, a weighty tome may signal that serious editing may be required, or that the author has failed to adhere to the principle of parsimony. Extra-long papers may be flawed in one of many ways: having a lack of focus or too many foci; redundancy, and unnecessary or extended references (beyond the works cited). In some cases, an abbreviated form of one's dissertation has been submitted without the necessary crystallization of ideas, tight editing, and reorganization required for a journal article.

Incubation is key: Put aside your drafts and reread them after a delay. Mull over your writing during periods of relaxation. Pajares (2004) reminds us that time and reflection are synthetic. This requires that you make good use of time and that you do not leave manuscript preparation until the last minute. You will catch sloppy writing and ugly proofreading errors by taking the extra time. Bring excellent copyeditors and proofreaders on board to assist you. Early in your scholarly career, it is wise to only submit manuscripts for publication after colleagues with reliable proofreading skills have vetted them.

Finally, anticipate the work of your reviewers. If editors will provide their rating sheets in advance, write your paper or revise it while consulting the journal's assessment criteria. Because few prospective authors ask for this form, some editorial staff will not be used to this request and may not comply. Criteria on the rating forms we have studied list overall originality of the work, relevance to the journal's scope and purpose, audience appeal, clarity and rigor of conceptual framework, sound discussion of the methods and procedures used, thorough analysis of the results obtained, and proper technical formatting and correct length. Turn the rating form into a checklist (the other one we recommended developing is the submission guidelines checklist). Learn to identify your own work's strengths and weaknesses. Remedy where you can and address all omissions. These extra efforts will go a long way toward securing a positive response to your work.

58   CAREFULLY PREPARE YOUR COVER LETTER AND SUMMARY

The author's cover letter, sometimes referred to as an overview, accompanies each manuscript submission. Carefully attend to the editor's manuscript preparation instructions and address these in your cover letter. If you're uncertain about any of these, contact the editor or editorial assistant, or ask an informed colleague. Because editors and addresses change, we recommend that you refer to the journal's Website or the most recent issue of the journal to confirm accuracy before sending your precious manuscript off—it will save you time and agony. In your cover letter, include a statement that briefly describes the "fit" between the work you are submitting and the journal. Clarify that your paper follows the journal's guidelines and be specific about how. Once you have submitted the package (cover letter, original manuscript, and requisite number of copies) to the editor, your manuscript is deemed "under submission." It's not considered "in review" until you receive word that the editor has moved ahead with the next stage, having secured reviewers. Do not send your manuscript elsewhere for review; it is an egregious ethical violation within the academy to submit the same work to more than one publication outlet simultaneously. It would be better for you to show up naked to class than to violate this time-honored convention. Where electronic submissions of cover letters are permitted, these can be handled as a separate file or, alternatively, within the e-mail message itself.

After the reviews are returned and the editor formulates a decision, you will receive word about the status of your work. Because few manuscripts are accepted after the first review, you should consider it good news if a manuscript is not rejected outright! When an editor offers a "conditional acceptance," "accept with changes," or a "revise and resubmit" decision, you have a proverbial foot in the door. Now, it is up to you to thoroughly address the feedback received from reviewers and editors as you carefully craft a revised manuscript.

Once you are confident that you have completely responded to the editor's recommendations and the reviewers' concerns, it's time to prepare a new letter to the editor. This is called the summary of changes cover letter. This detailed summary can be prepared in letter form and it accompanies the submission of the revised paper. Some writers include examples of changes, along with page numbers, directly in the letter, while others prepare generic statements that describe the changes made. Most editors do not specify the level of detail to be addressed in your summary of changes, so ask if necessary. In this case it's better to opt for more detail than less. In order to help the manuscript reach its full potential as a published work, take seriously all of the suggested changes. Address each requested change in your summary, organized by way of editor and reviewer, and justify any changes not made (don't just skip over them).

Some editors help authors approach the rewrite: Overarching goals or questions, as well as strategies for dealing with conflicting recommendations, can sometimes be found in their letters. Or they might reinforce what the reviewers have said; perhaps you will need to sharpen the work's focus, improve its organization, or explain its significance, for example. You might be only a revision away from publication acceptance or it may take several rigorous rewritings. Even though we are experienced authors, we continue to encounter both scenarios. One of us recently completed four separate revisions of a single brief article over the span of two-and-a-half years before it was finally published. Sometimes this level of demand has more to do with the editor's own standards or gatekeeping than with the quality of your revisions, but certainly not always. Hopefully, the revised manuscript will be significantly improved over the earlier version and the work will be ready to go to press; however, as frequently happens, when substantial revisions are undertaken, new weaknesses, as well as new opportunities for improvement, are exposed.

We suggest that you ask academic peers for summaries of changes as well as cover letters they have put together as samples to follow. Maintain a professional attitude toward the work and distance yourself from any feelings of personal insult. We often say that we must have grown "a new brain" in the time between submission and revision—the problems with the original draft seem obvious by then and the changes to be made come easily.

Here is a final word: Exercise patience during the entire publishing cycle and treat it as a great and even privileged learning opportunity: Stay focused on what matters—your continual growth as a professional writer, the quality of your product and message, and the contribution you will be making to an enduring public conversation.

59   CAREFULLY PREPARE YOUR BOOK PROSPECTUS

As with academic journals, carefully follow book publishers' submission guidelines, typically posted online. If not, contact the acquisitions editor and request that current guidelines be sent to you. Book proposal guidelines vary even more widely than journal guidelines; recognize that publisher guidelines range according to each publishing company's specific interests and needs. Here is one common denominator: Publishers focus on the marketing strengths of a work—after all, book publishers are in the business of making a profit. Acquisitions and managing editors have said that prospective authors have the most difficulty learning to appreciate and critically analyze market, competition, and audience. So you will want to pay particular attention to these related areas.

About the marketing of your book, here are some relevant questions to address: Who will buy your book? Who will be most interested in using your book, and how will they use it? Are they undergraduate students, graduate students, school administrators, clinical psychologists, classroom teachers, curriculum coordinators, researchers, staff developers, or some combination of the above? Might it appeal across academic disciplines? Could the book also find a niche with the general population? These are important marketing questions for you to consider and address in the prospectus.

Book publishers warn that authors must keep their audience in mind as they write—successful authors write for specific readers. Demonstrate that you have your readers fully within view even at the proposal stage. A common problem is to assume too little or too much prior knowledge of the subject area on the reader's part, or assume incorrectly what readers will do with the knowledge they acquire from the book. Avoid these pitfalls.

It has been our experience (having previously authored 16 books) that publishers will generally request that your prospectus address the following generic categories:

1. *brief description* of the proposed work, including a particular perspective or philosophical orientation
2. *competition* with respect to any primary competitors (other books on the topic)
3. *specific features* governing your work that will help it to stand apart and benefit users
4. *apparatus,* meaning the specifics that will enable your work to function as a learning tool (e.g., chapter questions, a glossary, chapter overviews)
5. *status of the work* with regard to its current development and your timeline for completion
6. *length of the book,* that is, a rough idea of the total manuscript length, which is much longer than the published book length
7. *table of contents* outlining your proposed organization of the work
8. *sample chapters* revealing the message, tone, and substance of the book.

Publishers want to see if you can write well, so they will ask for at least two sample chapters to be submitted for review along with your proposal. Novice writers are often expected to provide more material than experienced authors. At this stage, publishers may not want to receive the introductory chapters, as these tell rather than show what your book will do. It can take anywhere from two to five months for a book proposal to be reviewed, generally less time than it takes a refereed journal! However, this timeline can change depending on how many levels of evaluation are incorporated into the review process. The most prestigious book companies tend to incorporate at least three levels of review, with external reviewers (paid scholars), editorial board teams, and other screening partners, such as the publisher's marketing representatives, involved in the decision making. And contrary to the marked emphasis journal editors place on author anonymity, book publishers usually reveal your name and affiliation when sending your work for review. There is a reason for this exposure: Your name, track-record as a scholar, and even your institution's prestige can all play a role in a book's eventual success. Let's face it, name recognition is important in marketing any product—books are no exception. Another distinction is that, unlike journal manuscripts, you are allowed to simultaneously distribute your book proposal to other publishers. But it's considered good practice to make this fact known in your cover letter.

Always contact the acquisitions editor or whoever is in charge of author queries *before* tackling your proposal or book chapters. Of course, you can first try e-mailing these busy professionals, but count on having to follow up with a telephone call. In your conversation, float your idea and see what happens. Be flexible and receptive; an editor will often have a much better grasp of the market—even relative to your discipline—than you do. Sometimes an acquisitions editor will recommend a modification in your focus or your proposed approach. Take this advice to heart and make sure it is addressed in your written proposal.

Here is another crucial tip for successfully making contact with publishers: At the academic conferences you attend, spend time in the book exhibit. Acquisitions editors often "man" these exhibits and attend conferences for the express purposes of meeting with authors and exploring hot topical trends in their field. Seek out these important gatekeepers and share your ideas with them. If possible, make an appointment ahead of time to discuss your specific book idea. If well received, clarify the steps involved in preparing a thorough book prospectus. You will find these individuals generally receptive—many are author-centered and ready to hear from you. Without book authors they have no product to market. Savvy authors who have published a book or another significant work are often aware of conferences that will sponsor their work months in the future, so you, too, will want to be aware of the timing of your own book release.

After you have made contact with a book publisher, anything can happen from there: They might think the book idea is promising and that it potentially fits their needs, or instead that it does not fill any important gap in their booklist. Here's a sophisticated strategy that we employ: Study a selected publisher's catalogue and identify gaps that exist or areas that need developing. Because they are not academic scholars, publishers can be unaware of the weaknesses in their booklists. Turn your research knowledge and insights into a publishing strategy. Initiate this win/win exchange: If you can identify an opening in a publisher's catalogue *and* explain how your book proposal fills the void, you will have established a rationale for its support. This is how the book you are reading came to life, in fact—we could see from having researched Palgrave Macmillan's booklists that a text on prolific writing was needed to assist novice academics, and so we volunteered to write it *before* undergoing formal review. Many seasoned book authors bring such sensibilities to book publishing and negotiate ideas with editors early on, even before putting pen to paper. Successful book writing is about research, negotiation, relationship, reliability, and timeliness, not just a great idea.

From the editor who has reviewed your work for the publishing house, you should receive reviews and a statement about the viability of your work. If you get a "green light," move onto negotiating the contract. Talk to seasoned book writers about appropriate terms and royalties, which are usually less impressive for the first-time book writer. As examples, royalties on books sold tend to be lower and such perks as monetary advances are not usually negotiable. Novice writers are often expected to produce their own camera-ready pages as well, especially with smaller publishing companies. We have jumped through all of these hoops and more to get our first book contracts. If you have a winning book idea and the tenacity to see a mammoth project through, then start tinkering with a table of contents and a book prospectus. Think about publishers that might be a good fit and send an e-mail or two to acquisitions editors to begin exploring the viability of your idea. A book is a gargantuan scholarly undertaking, so you'd better get started sooner rather than later!

60   COMMUNICATE CLEARLY WITH EDITORS AND PUBLISHERS

Learning how to communicate clearly and effectively with editors and publishers is essential to a rising scholar's success. As one tip, alert these professionals to your intention of submitting a manuscript for review. Be prepared to succinctly describe your project: Seize the opportunity to receive helpful advice. Ask editors directly where you might go if your work is not a good fit with their press.

As a new scholar, you can also inquire about any special provisions for those who are beginners. For example, will you be promptly informed if the package you have submitted for review is incomplete? Or, will copyediting services be provided for works accepted for publication with journal or book presses? Although unusual, journal editors have been known to arrange it so that faculty mentors work with novice writers on the scholarly aspects of their writing.

People in editorial positions can be very difficult to reach, even by way of e-mail, but try anyway. Their assistants are usually reachable, though. Consult with editorial staff about the technical aspects of your work and straightforward matters regarding submission. Three examples are the approximate time for manuscript review, the planning of any special issues, and the status of your review. As the "worker bees," they tend to know about such particulars; editors handle more complex questions, such as the potential fit of your work with the journal, special issue, or booklist, as well as those publishing outlets that may be more appropriate for your work. Importantly, editors make final assessments of your revised journal manuscript or book proposal. Committed editorial assistants will communicate with editors on your behalf where necessary and get back to you. Editors and their assistants appreciate thoughtful queries. Author queries that tend to annoy editors involve requests for information that is readily available (e.g., posted/published submission guidelines) or attempts at negotiating required document formats (e.g., the American Psychology Association, the *Chicago Manual of Style*, the publisher's own in-house style). In contrast, updates during the review stage are usually welcome. Let editors know whether you will be proceeding with a revision once you've had the chance to reflect on the reviews. This information is not an imposition—it helps publishers with good planning. Also let them know whether the reviews proved useful. Here is an example of just such a message from an author.

Dear editor:

Just wanted to let you know that I've received all of your responses and plan to address them shortly. If I run into any difficulty, I'll let you know. I appreciate your continued efforts on my part and feel encouraged by the insightful reviews. I'll make the necessary changes and have the revised file to you within the month. I will be sure to send my summary of changes, as per your request.

Sometimes authors want to discuss, with the editor, the feedback they received from reviewers; at such times, you should clarify your concerns and seek strategies for dealing with discrepant or difficult feedback. For instance, authors are sometimes asked to increase their subject pool in order to better substantiate the claims they have made or to reformulate key arguments or recommendations. If you are unable to act on a key editorial or reviewer recommendation, prepare a justification and send it to the editor; on critical issues, come to an agreement before investing time in the rewrite.

Incorporate editors and publishers into your community of writers. While decision makers and gatekeepers, they are more productively thought of as professional colleagues. Approach them as human beings who are providing an invaluable service to the academy. As your own career matures and you begin to assume more editorial responsibility yourself, you may be surprised to discover that editors think of authors as valued colleagues. Return the favor now.

11

DRINK DEEPLY FROM
THE CUP OF LIFE

As scholars, our life experiences are not cut off from our writing; in fact, they can be used as a tool to explicitly frame and shape our works. Life-infused creativity can help you to foster connections between your writing and the rest of your life. What we learn in our daily living, and in life more generally, influences our writing—it is an art to give this reality form. You will also want to practice, as a busy academic, self-care and healthy habits, knowing that writing pressures can take a toll on one's health. Herein we share self-care strategies for writers. We also advocate bringing to life one's guiding philosophy in scholarly projects, including materials developed for tenure-and-promotion. The more time we spend in the academy, the more life-and-death experiences we will have, and so we need to learn how to gracefully weather these while maintaining our identity as a writer. In this chapter we reflect on this topic and provide strategies close to our own hearts. On a related note, we will all have to adapt to midlife as part of the process of aging; well-prepared writers are able to reduce negative outcomes associated with critical life transitions and enhance their chances for continued learning and growing.

61   CONNECT WRITING TO LIFE
AND LIFE TO WRITING

When your life experiences somehow enter into and shape the substance, meaning, or even style of your writing, expect your works to take on richer textures. Promote the connection between work and life in your own scholarship: Your positive writing experiences and relationships can create space for balance and wisdom. By immersing yourself in the stories of self and other, you'll have considerable fodder for illustrative examples and powerful experiential metaphors. Where one feels enlivened as a writer, writing can bring balance and texture to life (institutional service, availability to students, interactions with colleagues, and so on). Although it may seem that writing technical research reports offers little room for the life-infused creativity we encourage here, you might just find that these connections make even empirical writing more relevant and interesting.

When possible treat life itself as the material for academic writing. As one prolific scholar shared with us, "it may be that the best writing (maybe not the most, but the best) comes from those who have immersed themselves deeply in the living of life" (March 2006, personal communication). Healthy relationships focused on writing will naturally accommodate the worlds of reading, talking, and sharing where individuals enjoy one another's company. Reading circles and cohorts are potentially such places.

We who are professors and students experience "life" in the academy. Where relevant and appropriate, import the insights gained from your research, teaching, and service activities into your writing. You also experience "life" outside the academy through such contexts as family, marriage, and community. Once again, reflect on what you are learning, experiences you are weathering, and relationships you are savoring. What can these teach you about communicating with others as a writer? Seek ways to connect writing to life and life to writing. As examples, illustrations from writer's childhoods, child-rearing, illnesses, love relationships, and aging have all made their way into academic articles published in mainstream journals. Rites of passage throughout life and in the academy, and stories of loss and transition, also show up in many publications. A third example is the struggle writers have with personal and political identity, and the related issues of race and gender, tolerance and acceptance. The academic paradigm has changed considerably in recent years—it now accommodates personal, metaphoric, and mythological explorations of a deeper nature, as well as reflections and anecdotes that personalize one's inquiry. (Indeed, the journey motif has become so common it is a writer's cliché.) Look for venues that welcome experimentation with tradition—genre and form, and style and voice have taken a creative turn. Many of us find these openings not just intellectually rewarding but spiritually renewing.

Outrageously prolific educators see it as an advantage when the line between their professional and personal responsibilities, or their work and their play, disappears. For them, life and writing are seamless. In the field of education, John Goodlad, John Hoyle, Joseph Murphy, and Thomas Sergiovanni, along with many other scholars, believe that junior faculty must be passionate about and committed to their writing as their life's work (Mullen, 2006). When academics feel such passion, work and play become entangled, lessening the burden of work.

Sergiovanni's passionate capacity translates into having a "laser-like focus" and being "protective" of his time yet generous toward helping students with their programs and projects. Goodlad's tendency to ask fascinating questions, model inquiry in groups, and collaborate on issues involving educational change are all sources of passion. Murphy, a "very disciplined writer," can work "completely unruffled all day long"; he also imbues passion in students by having them focus on their own development as scholars and by reflecting on the kinds of lifelong contributions they might make to education. Hoyle experiences a "white heat" when writing, and he encourages students and leaders to take a strong position on educational issues while shining light on others' contributions. He notes that "I have a sense of having to get certain words out. I hammer away, and it's amazing what happens when you get into that white heat." When his mental energy coalesces, a significant work, even an entire book, will "just pour out." He works "like crazy to get something out of my head that needs to get out" (Mullen, 2006, p. 14).

For an excellent model of experience-infused writing, consider the inspiring work of John Dewey. Its poetic, meditative voice helps us to imagine ourselves in a place where everything is growing, and where we can SEE HEAR FEEL growth.

Positive growth is patterned activity without beginning or end—texture, density, and depth all infuse the writer's life. Be radiant—embrace growth that nourishes connections between writing and life, life and writing.

62   PRACTICE SELF CARE
AND HEALTHY HABITS

Committed academics frequently struggle with "workaholic" tendencies and the accompanying toll this inevitably takes on one's health (emotionally, physically, and existentially). Amid all of the responsibilities and pressures of writing, awareness of your own needs can seem selfish, frivolous, or merely too time consuming.

However, academic writers who respect their own needs are generally able to function at a higher level than those who do not. This is particularly important to remember during the various crises we face in academe (e.g., unexpected assignments, impossible deadlines, the looming specter of promotion and tenure), when it is easy to ignore your own needs. Don't wait for a crisis to occur before establishing healthy habits. Begin seeking balance and maintaining yourself physically and emotionally early in your career. This practice will evolve into a life-long habit and more than likely enhance your longevity as a writer.

There are a range of ways to relieve stress by recharging your battery—celebrations, retreats, workshops, nature walks, hiking, gardening, motivational tapes, exercise, and a healthy diet, to name a few. Anyone who cares about your well-being and from whom you seek confidential advice can be an energizer too. Cathartic conversations with trusted colleagues can make a big difference. Meditation, yoga, prayer, napping, art, cultural events, meals with friends, courses, travel, and pleasure reading can also be essential energizers. Find ways to "recharge" your personal and professional battery every day and try helping others to do the same. Even relatively minor efforts can go a long way toward promoting a healthy mind and body.

How have your authors managed to practice routine self-care? I (Carol) routinely spend time each week at the gym using the cardio and weight machines and also jogging in the neighborhood. I have been exercising since I was a young teen while running track and so I have a workout habit, although I got away from my commitment while tenure-earning and suffered for it. I spend time refueling by working in the garden at home, traveling locally and overseas to favorite and unfamiliar places, and arranging to meet special colleagues at conferences. I enjoy my face-to-face and electronic communications with colleagues who have become good friends, and I cherish the joy they bring me. All appreciate writing, relationships, and travel, and all are soulful, humorous beings who shed light on weighty issues.

I (Brad) allot an hour-and-a-half each day around the lunch hour to go running or swimming. At the Naval Academy, exercise is a cultural expectation and it has become an automatic life habit for me. I also strive to be home at a reasonable hour each day so that I can take advantage of spending quality (and quantity) time with my three teenage sons—I find our times together to be deeply satisfying. Finally, I maintain frequent contact with good friends and colleagues—most of whom share my interest in writing and appreciate my dry sense of humor. Humor can be remarkably rejuvenating on many levels.

Here is a sober observation regarding the writing life: Extended periods of long-duration writing can promote overeating, poor eating, unwanted weight gain, and fatigue. Many of us fight these demons every day. Not only is the act of writing itself inherently sedentary, periods of high-tempo writing (often spurred by approaching deadlines or increasing anxiety about departmental evaluation) can cause disregard for even well-established healthy habits. Just as writing should be a daily regimen, so should caring for yourself.

Here are some specific strategies for promoting good health even in the face of a demanding writing schedule. Keep in mind that each of these habits is additive—healthy behaviors tend to promote other healthy behaviors. First, consider that stretching can be incorporated with relative ease right at your computer! Tennis elbow exercises are a great way to give relief to your hands and arms while taking momentary breaks. One of us asked a tennis pro to show us the proper way to stretch our extremities and tendons; the daily exercises help mitigate the effects of tendonitis, caused by repetition of small motor movements (typing). Move around in your office to give relief to your neck, upper back, and lower back—all writers' ailments. Why wait for that seemingly elusive "perfect" time to exercise? You don't even have to leave your office or home to get some relief. Or, consider joining a weight-training program at your university or in your community: Ask about cost-free programs with intern trainers. Trainers will create a custom-made routine for you, and monitor your progress while giving your writing muscles a good workout!

Be deliberate about your diet. We know far too many college professors who continue to eat (and sometimes act) like college students. When ensconced in a writing jag it is all too easy to make the building's vending machine your prime source of sustenance or to eat sugary snacks that mysteriously appear in the departmental lounge. Don't do it! Plan your eating regimen carefully. We recommend packing your food for the day at a time when you are not hungry (prior to bed the night before). Include two or more small healthy meals rather than one large high-caloric feast, and include snacks consisting of items like fruit, carrot sticks, or trail mix. Also, have plenty of water on hand. Research indicates that dehydration is pervasive and often causes sensations of hunger and fatigue—keep hydrated.

Remember, the better you get at living the writing life, the more natural it will be to practice self-care while being productive. It may be that when writers separate these two worlds—writing and self-care—both or either suffers. You can easily "write in your head," so to speak, during just about any activity, including exercise and eating. When the act of creating scholarship is a joy and a vocation, you will often find yourself unconsciously strategizing and outlining current or future projects as you exercise or play. We think this is good! But keep things in perspective and recognize that writing can also be very hard work that places demands on the physical self. Tenure-earning faculty are especially challenged by the demand to balance productivity and self-care. The academy's emphasis on refereed publication can feel like an inescapable mantra—produce, produce, produce!

We've noticed that, despite aging issues, many tenured faculty manage to establish a healthy work/life equilibrium that often escapes their junior colleagues. If repression and sacrifice define the tenure-earning faculty's life, balance and wisdom define their senior colleague's. While an overstatement, this has a kernel of truth. Test it out for yourself. Ask prolific scholars you know whether they've managed to achieve balance and wisdom in their work lives, post-tenure, and, if so, how? Is it possible that some of these strategies could be employed early in your career to good effect? While you don't want to spend your life on a golf course or in a shopping mall, learn what you can about the intricate balancing routines of prolific colleagues that could improve your life. And here is one more observation about prolific academics. Rarely does achieving tenure result in a marked slowdown in their scholarly output. Because writing is deeply interwoven with their identities, and because they love to create, the idea of discontinuing the writing is nearly inconceivable. This is also why balancing life, health, and scholarship is a natural for these scholars—they're in this for the long-haul.

We both have regular writing-and-exercise routines, and active networks with collegial friends. Excitement for us also comes in the form of breakthrough ideas for new projects; we seek out collaboration with committed colleagues like ourselves. We drink deeply from the cup of life and in such places as professional meetings, where our batteries are recharged, as old friendships are awakened and new ones formed. And both of us look for opportunities to play hard—even in the midst of scheduled professional tasks. For instance, Brad recently gave a talk at Pearl Harbor, Hawaii, on leadership and mentoring. So, he did the only logical thing a fun-loving dad could do: he took his youngest son along to go surfing during his off-hours. Carol has gone swimming with stingrays and written poetry about the experience, later published in an academic journal.

Last, seek equilibrium between work and life, and develop healthy routines and writing habits. Practice self-care every day.

63   INFUSE YOUR WRITING WITH
A GUIDING PHILOSOPHY

One way to drink deeply from the cup of life is to infuse your writing with a guiding philosophy—a personally meaningful view of life and the place of your scholarship within it. Writing that has a clear philosophical foundation will bring coherence to each new project as well as your overall work; it will become the undergirding structure for each of your contributions. Tenure-and-promotion is a time when candidates are expected to share their guiding philosophies of research and teaching. Having a lucid philosophical foundation that is reinforced daily is essential for experiencing success and deriving a sense of meaning from your work. Because academics are attracted to complicated words, it is imperative to state your guiding philosophy in a simple phrase and try it out around others. As an example, "I believe that all school reform should be in the interest of student learning and their role in society as democratic citizens." If effective, this philosophy should easily form the substrate for meaningful theory, research, and application.

A philosophy is a worldview supported by beliefs; these can be written out as statements. Your beliefs, once articulated, will help you continually examine your practice. Whereas some of us are attracted exclusively to empirically-derived principles, others may feel compelled by stories of experience or even spiritual or religious explanations of life. Whatever the source of your beliefs and daily practices, articulate them clearly and consider their congruence with other important intellectual and personal commitments.

Once you've developed a philosophy for guiding your work, you will be clearer about which writing opportunities make sense to pursue now or later and which should be avoided altogether. You will also want to develop some overriding themes that give "personality" to your work, in addition to a set of ethics that might possibly underpin all your efforts. Ask yourself who you are and what you stand for as a writer, and what kind of difference you want to make. Take control of your many clever ideas. Give them a recognizable form.

Let's consider a philosophy of inaction: A college professor who is committed to researching disadvantaged school settings and moral attitudes toward and within them has found a way to mesh her philosophy with her research. In one such school led by an exemplary principal, it became evident that theories of human development, including Abraham Maslow's

Hierarchy of Needs model (physiological, safety, social, and esteem), guided the administrators and teachers' decision making. The professor was pleased to see that all curricular programs and major school decisions were shaped around this tenet. And she appreciated the difficult journey the school had taken to eliminate ineffective programs and to transfer culturally insensitive teachers. The adults at this highly impoverished school believed that children could not be expected to learn, or be taught—including tested on standardized exams—until their basic needs were met. Curricular and instructional improvements mattered only when basic needs were satisfied and on an ongoing basis. In her analysis of the school's leadership, philosophy, and programs, the researcher discussed the commitment of transformational leaders to values centered on child advocacy and social justice, and to actions that focus on not just what works but what is good. In the manuscript that was developed, moral action and leadership informed the school's collective actions in support of child advocacy and social justice.

Thinking today about your future life work, where and how do you want to leave your mark? What will your legacy be? What issues, causes, and concerns stimulate you to action? Use these questions to begin crystallizing your belief statements; from there, develop a guiding philosophy. Permeate your writing with this highly personal worldview and alter it as your thinking changes. It will become more sophisticated and perhaps influential the more you share it.

Don't forget to study the philosophy or mission of your institution, college, and department. Reflect on the extent to which your outlook coincides with the institution's. Don't wait until you are putting together your promotional packages to discover glaring conflicts; be thoughtful and transparent about how you resolve them. Address any overlaps and gaps in your scholarly statements. Overlaps project a healthy picture, suggesting that the focus you bring to your work has been institutionally validated; gaps can also be good. They may indicate that you are offering something new and special to your workplace. Prepare for this political form of writing early on as a new faculty member.

No doubt, our philosophies are an integral part of who we are as educators. Take this book, for example. Explicit is our belief that novice writers can learn from the attitudes and practices of experienced scholars. We also believe that the act of writing for publication is such a challenge that it must be broken down into digestible elements. Further, we believe that the truly productive academic integrates writing into the fabric of his or her life, and that for the outrageously prolific academic, writing is a personal, vocational, spiritual, recreational, and a lifelong commitment.

Make your writing true to your philosophy and view of the world.

64   GRACEFULLY WEATHER CRITICAL LIFE EVENTS

At times—often just when you have established a productive writing groove—life intrudes. External events grab our attention, create powerful emotional experiences, and force us to step back from writing to take stock, and to care for ourselves and others. While critical life events may actually help us as writers to create anew, absorbing the energy of shock, loss, hope, and recovery can also take a serious toll. Major life-and-death experiences encompass the birth of a child and the death of a loved one, such as a parent or partner. In addition to birth and death, other larger-than-life events include marriage, breakups, health problems (physical and psychological), conflicts with children or family members, and, as discussed in the following section, existential crises. For some, even the death of someone unknown to them, yet symbolically important, can lead to a period of intense grieving—consider the classic cases of Diana, Princess of Wales, John Lennon, and certainly President John Kennedy. Even over long periods of time, entire communities and countries have been known to mourn the loss of one collectively loved.

Whether these critical life events involve joyous occasions or painful occurrences, and whether they are sudden or slow to unfold, the question for the prolific scholar is this: How can you gracefully weather these inevitable life experiences while maintaining your fundamental identity as a writer? How can you thoughtfully consider your own work in light of the real events you are living?

It is essential to our own health and well-being as academic writers to take time to grieve, to count our blessings, to reconnect with loved ones, and even to reconsider our personal and professional choices—all the while continuing to live fully and honor obligations to others and ourselves. Critical life events rarely permit expeditious resolution; rather, they are characteristically lifelong journeys through which grieving, longing, and remembrance can take different forms over time; acceptance and peace are among the hoped-for outcomes. In the case of loss, rituals can certainly help with the healing process, offering a personal or corporate avenue to openly express our feelings and to remember the one who has departed. In *The Lovely Bones*, novelist Sebold (2002) describes the annual ritual of community mourning that took place as friends and family members would gather in a cornfield at night with lit candles to sing and pray together. Writers have rituals as well. Some of us use the acknowledgement and dedication pages of books to express gratitude for those living and deceased who have shaped our lives. Others of us may focus our scholarship on issues or events that have hit close to home (e.g., autism, cancer, loss of a child, dissolution of a marriage). We encourage you to consider rituals that facilitate integrating the delights and losses life sends your way.

Obviously, the feelings of rejoicing and experiences of celebration that accompany birth are very different from those of pain and loss accompanying death. But remember that joyous occasions can rival death and loss in terms of the costs they exact from your time and energy. For example, the responsibility that accompanies raising a newborn, and the excitement and anxiety, including sleeplessness, that go hand-in-hand with having a baby in the home will markedly affect one's writing routine. Reactions to the death of a loved one vary, as we may despair more in the case of a child or young person, or even a healthy adult. But even the passing of an older adult who has been ill for some time and who has prepared for death can be overwhelming, especially with the grieving that accompanies a significant loss and the energy that is required to extend oneself in different directions, which only perpetuates diminished practices of self-care.

As academics who write and must do so, the question becomes, How can you accept, tolerate, and eventually adapt to critical life events, giving permission for some slowdown in your writing while not letting it go altogether? There are no easy answers. During the writing of this particular secret Carol had just experienced the loss of her 67-year-old father for whom the diagnosis of widespread cancer one year earlier had surprised even his doctors. She learned all over again just as she had with the passing of her mother years earlier that while academic writing per se is not necessarily healing for her, the act of being absorbed in something meaningful proved therapeutic, just as is keeping busy, whether it be with gardening, reading, or walking, and welcoming the love and concern of family and friends. All such activity can help with surviving the initial feelings of numbness and disbelief, and experiences of insomnia and disorientation.

Life-enriching experiences, such as the arts, crafts, gardening, and gatherings, can certainly help grieving individuals feel connected as they breathe new life into their lives and selves. We know a professor whose entire family turned to the arts, not just for exposure but for ongoing participation in theatrical performances, initially as a way of dealing with the loss of several loved ones. He shared that the arts have produced a synergistic bond among his wife, children, himself, and theatrical performers and entire communities, and that highly positive emotional, social, and cognitive outcomes have been realized for all of the actors, including his six-year-old son.

With the loss of her dearly loved father, Carol gave herself permission to approach her writing differently, especially given the sudden emotional needs of her brother and sister. Her life changed overnight, placing her, as the first born, in a clear parental role with respect to her younger siblings, suddenly at a loss with both parents deceased. Regarding productivity, during this trying time in her life, Carol was able at first to attend to e-mail and postal mail only. Then, within a short time, she built up to responsibilities with respect to the editing and guest editing of two different academic journals and eventually returned to writing projects that required revision. She found it too difficult at first to write anything from scratch, as the intellectual energy level required tends to be much more demanding than for works needing revision.

To the extent possible, it may be wise to plan in advance of critical life events where these are anticipated, such as, when possible, completing projects demanding original research and writing before the event occurs. Of course, life is rarely so neat and "schedule-friendly," but if you anticipate the death of a loved one or your child's marriage, plan well in advance to stand-down from your writing schedule. Give yourself ample time to celebrate, grieve, and generally experience the textures of thought and emotion that accompany these events and have the power to make you more mature as a human being and scholar.

If you can, continue with writing even if in very modest forms during the time of change. If not, engage in relaxing activities that have healing or at least absorbing powers for you. You may already know what level and type of writing you are capable of when faced with critical life experiences. You never know what activities will end up feeding your writer's mind when you are not even thinking about your writing and productivity!

65 ADAPT AT MIDLIFE (AND BEYOND)

In addition to the salient life events and crises that punctuate our writing careers, there are likely to be less sharply defined "seasons" and transitions as we learn and mature. For instance, the early career or young adulthood phase is characterized by energy, excitement, and seemingly unbounded promise. New professors scramble to find a focus, achieve early career success, and formulate a career dream. And of course the end-of-career phase of a scholar's life carries its own need for meaning-making. Professors nearing retirement are often focused on reflecting, taking stock of their professional careers, and deciding if and how to continue engagement with the task of writing. But perhaps the most important life phase for the typical

academic—and the one we address as we wrap up this guide—
is the infamous *midlife* transition. The transition from young
adulthood to midlife can be gradual or abrupt, barely percep-
tible or deeply troubling. One thing is certain: You need to be
deliberate and intentional in preparing for this shift if you
want to reduce negative outcomes and enhance your chances
of learning and growing from this change in your own
scholarly life.

There is a proverb that goes, "Midlife is the old age of youth
and the youth of old age." If true, then many academics are
standing on the threshold of a new youth. The demographic
shift in society—many of us now live and continue to work well
into our 80s and 90s—extends to the academic realm. Take a
look around your own department and you may witness the
"graying" of the professorate. Many of us have excellent models of older colleagues who remain sharp, active, and even prolific well beyond midlife. Thus, in many ways, midlife may
portend the start of a long, stable, and creative phase of life. In
New Passages, Sheehy (1996) refers to midlife as the *second
adulthood*. For many adults, midlife offers a rare opportunity
for a second shot at becoming the sort of person, the sort of
partner, or the sort of scholar we were destined to be.

Following the storm and intensity of young adulthood and
early career, many of us have achieved tenure, been promoted,
and settled into a personal lifestyle that fits. We have often
achieved some comfort in our academic positions and hopefully
at least a modest degree of notoriety within the scholarly community. And then it happens. Slowly we begin to sense that we
are metamorphosing into a new stage of life—perhaps signaled
by career achievements, changes in family structure, the loss of
loved ones, or even changes in our own bodies. As scholars and
human beings we must be cautious and thoughtful about this
shift—accepting that it may be a time of both creative renewal
and dangerous behavior.

As a prolific academic, we encourage you to focus on the
promise and possibility of the midlife transition. Adaptive
midlife scholars use the onset of midlife as an opportunity to
slow down, take stock, and consider their career and life
involvements in light of earlier dreams and aspirations. Sheehy

(1996) notes that this is the time to jettison things we no longer need and focus in on projects, activities, and commitments that give us a powerful sense of purpose and focus—midlife can be an invitation to live the rest of our lives with renewed meaning and enjoyment. Midlife can be a time of personal renaissance and rejuvenation. In Baker's (1982) *Tolstoy's Bicycle*, we are treated to a description of Leo Tolstoy, the famous Russian novelist, who learned to ride a bicycle for the first time at age 67 and used his later life to find profound fulfillment in his spiritual life and writing. As you reflect on your own scholarly career at midlife—considering both the road behind you and the road ahead—it is important to ask whether you are teaching and writing about what moves you. Is this the work that you should be doing? Is your current writing stale or your focus of inquiry spiritually null? If so, what will you dare to do about it? At midlife, you have less to gain from making momentous changes, and much to lose from failing to seek congruence between your writing and your intellectual and personal passions.

Although an adaptive response to the inevitable changes of midlife will almost certainly enliven and reaffirm your identity as scholar, it is also true that some among us have a difficult time with this phase. Sheehy (1996) and others use the term *midlife crisis* to refer to the more precipitous and dramatic reactions that some adults manifest at this time. We are all familiar with a colleague who, in the throes of a dawning awareness of his or her own mortality, seem to react with defiant rebellion—perhaps impulsively divorcing a spouse, getting tattoos or excessive plastic surgery, buying a motorcycle, dating a student, and otherwise acting out at work. But such catastrophic reactions to aging are neither necessary nor likely for those who face midlife head-on by thoughtfully adjusting to their new physical, emotional, and relational realities. In the Chinese language, the ideogram for crisis is a combination of two distinct characters: One represents danger and the other, opportunity. From a Chinese perspective, then, midlife conjures the image of "dangerous opportunity."

As a busy academic, it is difficult to predict precisely what signs and signals may tilt you in the direction of processing your own midlife phase. Common catalysts include realization of a long-standing dream, shifts in location or lifestyle, or even baldness and weight gain! The key to an adaptive response seems to be the presence of a meaningful focus and direction in your work. Take Paul Gaugin, the French post-impressionist painter (1848–1903), for an example. Gaugin left a career in banking at the age of 46, and moved from Europe to Tahiti in order to live the painter's life. Throughout his early career, Gaugin had suppressed his long-standing dream of becoming an artist. In midlife, Gaugin began creating an unusual, avant-garde painting style that set the art world on a new course.

Assuming the broader, positive view for our purposes here, Gaugin's life can be contrasted with a negative midlife crisis. In the latter instance, one can picture a life of quiet desperation, symbolizing the French existentialist mindset that all roads lead to no exit. People with this outlook would have the profound sense that their life has been meaningless, that life is passing by because they lack a sense of direction, and that everything that has proceeded has been for naught. For academic writers, existential crises can be expressed in any number of subtle and not-so-subtle ways, as in the dawning realization that academic writing is not deeply or spiritually satisfying, or that one's writing is not being read or making any kind of discernible impact, or that writing is not one's forte after all. It is probably natural for academics to feel any and all such emotions at different times in our careers, especially in the face of a critical life event. Actually, it *is* difficult to know the extent to which one's writing and publications are making a difference, as it can take years before we have any clear idea.

Radical midlife changes and transitions are not just the stuff of myth and folklore. As a prominent contemporary example, consider the emergence of "second-career priests." These males, averaging 45 years old, are mature individuals who have held jobs, been in intimate relationships, and, often, raised families with their former spouses. Englert (2006) who wrote *The Collar*, spent a year in 2002 at Sacred Heart seminary outside Milwaukee documenting five of the seminary's older male students. He chronicled what they were learning through formal classes, and their conflicts and hopes. The author describes how second-career priests possess the gems of lived experience to offer their congregations; they can better relate to the problems people bring them than their traditional counterparts. Unlike many young people who choose this vocation, the older adults have given up the earthly life after having had, in some cases, satisfying secular lives. They describe their life change as a "calling" from outside and within, and share that life in its conventional forms could not sustain them (National Public Radio [NPR], 2006).

As a scholar, we encourage you to enter the challenging territory of midlife with eyes wide open: What made sense and what sustained you as a young adult may no longer work at midlife. In fact, the academy may no longer feel like home; writing as a way of life may no longer infuse your life with excitement and meaning. As you may well know, "no human activity can sap the strength from body and life from spirit as much as writing in which one doesn't believe" (Germano, 2006, p. B5). Alternatively, midlife may be a satisfying opportunity to affirm the path you are currently traveling as a writer and teacher—the midlife transition may simply be an opportunity to add new twists or creative angles to your scholarly landscape. On a more intensive scale, midlife may offer a greater opportunity than previous periods for the increasingly skilled academic writer to, metaphorically speaking, "imagine the mountain—conjure a subject and its dimension, envision its height, dream up the cloud cover" (Germano, 2006, p. B5). Unlike real mountain climbers, academic midlifers will want to imagine it anew and make the "climb" not because the mountain is there but because it isn't there and needs to be. Whatever your decision pathway, we hope midlife will afford you the chance to find a renewed sense of calling and direction in your work and life. Finally, we also hope that *Write to the Top!* has provided you with a view of the mountaintop that has proven well worth the climb.

References

Baker, J. (1982). *Tolstoy's bicycle*. New York: St. Martin's Press.

Boyer, E. L. (1990). *Scholarship reconsidered: Priorities of the professoriate.* New York: The Carnegie Foundations for the Advancement of Teaching.

de Janasu, S. C., & Sullivan, S. E. (2004). Multiple mentoring in academe: Developing the professorial network. *Journal of Vocational Behavior, 64,* 263–283.

Dillard, A. (1989). *The writing life.* New York: HarperPerennial.

Ellis, A. (1985). *Overcoming resistance: Rational-emotive therapy with difficult clients.* New York: Springer.

Englert, J. (2006). *The collar: A year of striving and faith inside a Catholic seminary.* Boston, MA: Houghton Mifflin.

Gaugin, P. (1997). *Gaugin's intimate journals.* New York: Dover Publications.

Germano, W. (2006, June 9). Why we write. *Chronicle of Higher Education, 52*(40), B5.

Glatthorn, A. A. (1998). *Writing the winning dissertation: A step-by-step guide.* Thousand Oaks, CA: Corwin.

Goleman, D. (1995). *Emotional intelligence.* New York: Bantam.

Henson, K. T. (1999). *Writing for professional publication: Keys to academic and business success.* Needham Heights, MA: Allyn & Bacon.

Hoyle, J. R. (1995). *Leadership and futuring: Making visions happen.* Thousand Oaks, CA: Corwin.

Jamison, K. R. (1996). *An unquiet mind: A memoir of moods and madness.* New York: Vintage.

Johnson, W. B., & Ridley, C. R. (2004). *The elements of mentoring.* New York: Palgrave Macmillan.

Kiernan, V. (2006, June 9). Toss out the index cards. *Chronicle of Higher Education, 52*(40), A29–30.

King, S. (2000). *On writing: A memoir of the craft.* New York: Scribner.

Lamott, A. (1994). *Bird by bird.* New York: Random House.

Lazarus, R. S., & Folkman, S. (1984). *Stress, appraisal, and coping.* New York: Guilford.

Massy, W. F., Wilger, A. K., & Colbeck, C. (1994). Overcoming "hallowed" collegiality. *Change, 26*, 10–20.

Messina, J. J., & Messina, C. M. (2006). *Coping.org: Tools for coping with life's stressors/tools for personal growth: Overcoming perfectionism.* Retrieved on March 12, 2006, from http://www.coping.org/growth/perfect.htm.

Mullen, C. A. (2005). *The mentorship primer.* New York: Peter Lang.

———, C. A. (2006). *A graduate student guide: Making the most of mentoring.* Lanham, MD: Rowman & Littlefield Education.

———, C. A. (2006, Fall). Exceptional scholarship and democratic agendas: Interviews with John Goodlad, John Hoyle, Joseph Murphy, and Thomas Sergiovanni. *NCPEA Connexions.* Connexions article/module (m14103) (available at www.cnx.org; search term "Mullen")

National Public Radio (NPR). *'Collar' tells story of one year, five seminarians.* (2006, April 16). [Jacki Lynden, host]. Audiorecording retrieved on April 17, 2006, from http://www.npr.org/templates/story/story.php?storyId=5344706

Pajares, F. (2004). The elements of a proposal (pp. 1–9). Retrieved on May 31, 2006, from http//:www.emory.edu/education/mfp/proposal.html.

Payne, R. K. (1998). *A framework for understanding poverty* (revised edition). Highlands, TX: RFT Publishing.

Peck, M. S. (1978). *The road less traveled.* New York: Touchstone.

Rheingold, H. L. (1994). *The psychologist's guide to an academic career.* Washington, DC: American Psychological Association.

Sebold, A. (2002). *The lovely bones.* New York: Little, Brown and Company.

Sheehy, G. (1996). *New passages.* New York: Ballantine Books.

Sternberg, R. J. (1986). A triangular theory of love. *Psychological Review, 93*, 119–135.

Strunk, W., & White, E. B. (2000). *The elements of style* (4th ed.). Boston, MA: Allyn & Bacon.

Thomas, P. L. (2005). *Teaching writing.* New York: Peter Lang.

Walen, S. R., DiGiuseppe, R., & Dryden, W. (1992). *A practitioner's guide to rational-emotive therapy* (2nd ed.). New York: Oxford.

Wikipedia, the free encyclopedia. (2006, May). *David Henry Thoreau.* Retrieved May 6, 2006, from http://en.wikipedia.org/wiki/Thoreau

Wolcott, H. (2001). *Writing up qualitative research* (2nd ed.). Thousand Oaks, CA: Sage.

INDEX